Numb

Surviving the Madness of the Iran Revolution...
A True Story in Tehran

Azita

Copyright © 2015 by Azita.

All rights reserved worldwide.
No part of this publication may be replicated, redistributed, or given away in any form without the prior written consent of the author/publisher or the terms relayed to you herein.

Azita
Azita Publishing

ISBN-13: 978-1508716396
ISBN-10: 1508716390

Life is a lot like riding on a train. We all share parts of our lives together as the passengers of the same moving power. If people smile by remembering you after you are gone, then you have achieved a positive life.

Table of Contents

Dedication 5
Prologue 7
Chapter One 23
   "I think they got him." 23
   Numb is Numb, is My Sword and Shield. 23
Chapter Two 27
   Polad 27
Chapter Three 33
   Family and Background Influences 33
   Childhood Memories 33
Chapter Four 59
   How Did it Happen? 59
Chapter Five 71
   Celebration Among the Turmoil 71
Chapter Six 85
   Married Life 85
Chapter Seven 89
   Changes – Living with a Revolutionist 89
Chapter Eight 95
   Wonderful News 95
Chapter Nine 101
   Challenges 101
Chapter Ten 111
   Free Falling on the Rocks (Numb Revisited) 111

Chapter Eleven 119
    Fun Life 119
    Ten Days after Polad was Captured 119
Chapter Twelve 135
    Where is My Husband? 135
Chapter Thirteen 139
    Surviving… 139
Chapter Fourteen 145
    Thirty Six Questions and Counting… 145
Chapter Fifteen 163
    The Road to Exile 163
Chapter Sixteen 181
    New Beginning 181
Epilogue and Legacy 195
Appendix 203
    Our House Rules while the children were growing up in the US .. 203

Dedication

I dedicate this memoir to my children who gave me reasons to live, at a time when I hardly felt any appreciation for being alive.

I also would like to dedicate my greatest gratitude to Sarah for making this book possible. I am grateful to my husband Rick for his understanding throughout the many years during my efforts of bringing my sweet and bitter memories onto paper, even some of those which I thought I had forgotten forever. We think that we have dealt with issues or buried them but at some point, up they crop again!

Last and not least, I would like very much to offer my sincere gratitude to HWB who reminded me that I still am a person with positive and negative feelings, and it is OKAY to be just a human.

I would also like to offer a few words to the burned generation of Iran. Those 30 and 40 year old young men and women who lived their entire childhood, teen years and young adulthood under the dictatorship of the barbaric Islamic government in Iran, which robbed our country of its true revolution towards a better life for all people, and turned it into a mockery of a two thousand year old religion. I know you all blame those of us who stood up to the Shah's government to provide education, housing and food for all Iranians, but in fact, and sadly, made things worse for you instead. Please forgive us and remember that the 1979 Iranian revolution was high-jacked from its true and sincere destination.

Azita at ages 14, 17 and then 27, after the revolution

Prologue

"If you are Iranian, why aren't you living there? Why are you here?"

When that question arises, this book will serve as the answer. That's why I'm sharing this story. This is for my children. They should know their heritage and how they came to reside in America. This is my contribution to posterity. This is for their children and the generations to come, as I'm sure that within the next two generations they won't be speaking Farsi at all. I sincerely hope that my children will continue recounting their heritage to their children, but the truth of the matter is that even my children don't really know that much. That is one important motive for the writing of this book.

What will happen if such memories are left to slip away? These memories can't be replaced once they've disappeared. These memories are standing up for love and justice. Few of us take the time to capture our memories as a legacy to not only our loved ones but the following generations. I realized that this was something for me to do and committed myself to the doing of it. I trust that you will agree with me when I say that family and love are the most important things in this world. In writing this memoir one of my aims is strengthening the bond between us by sharing information about the people who brought them into being. In so doing, I hope to bring us all a better sense of who we are. Apparently, I'm a torch bearer. There's one in every family.

This work also has the purpose of showing non-Iranians that what they see on the news – unfortunate people, especially women (covering themselves and walking behind men, deprived of their identity and individuality), or villages with bare-footed children wandering in the streets with runny noses and flies in their eyes – is not really Iran. Iran has been a combination of village, farm and city life. There were poor farmers, this is true, but in contrast, there were well-read, highly educated and fashion-conscious folk too. I think the world needs to realize all that, because the image people have of Iran and its people is not right or true. My passion is to reveal the true Iran.

This picture was taken back in 1952 in Iran. My mother was a school teacher and they used to take a group picture once a year. She is the fifth person sitting from the right. As you see, women didn't have any hair or full body covering, and were sitting next to men with no problem or hesitation.

So, I want people to see Iran and Iranians in a better light – not as better or worse people, but in a better light. Since I set foot on American soil I've told people about my life in Iran – what life was like for me and others there. When people talk about what they've seen on television I've often been heard, over the years, saying: "No, that's not what it's like." I've felt the need to justify why I don't want to hang my head low when I talk about being Iranian. It isn't all negative. There is beauty in Iran and the people of Iran. I want people to see through and past the fundamentalist regime and the Guardians of the Islamic Revolution…

Our family picture 1964, Tehran. My mother loved to push for family pictures every year. She would dress herself and us very elegantly for those pictures! In front of our parents, I am the one (with big ears!) on the left side of my mom, then my little sister and our brother.

Of course, it wasn't all roses in Iran before the new regime took over. Not everyone had a well-off life as my family did. I realize that, and that isn't what I'm saying. I can remember experiences to illustrate that too, and I'm not trying to cover that side of Iran up or gloss over it, but it wasn't the everyday norm. That is what I'd like to get across to you. In fact, at this moment, if you will permit me, I'd like to illustrate with one memory that profoundly touched my heart.

Why don't they have homes?

One cold morning in November, as I was driving on the highway outside of the City of Tehran, on my way to school, I noticed a child of about maybe 8 years old standing at the side of the highway. She was dressed "like gypsies" as we described it, a colorful top, short wavy skirt and a pair of pants under the skirt. Her face was small and red from the cold wind and her little body was being launched sideways as the cars were passing by at full speed. I pulled over and got out of the car and asked the child what she was doing there.

"My mom is sick; please help us." I don't remember if I locked the car doors or not, but I asked her to take me to her mother. She started walking away from the road, through the hills of snow and wet ground and I followed. As we were getting away from the highway I could hear sounds of whistling as if people were communicating with each other. Years later, I realized that what I did was not very wise considering the movements in

Iran at that time, and the hatred that needy people had developed towards the rich.

As we got far enough away from the road, I could see make-shift shelters made of old mattresses and pieces of cardboard around an open field. There were young boys all around this community who were whistling to announce the stranger's approach as we were getting closer. I followed the little girl into one of those shelters and as soon as my eyes could see in the dark, I noticed a very thin young woman who was lying on a pile of rags on the floor, in the corner. Her face looked extremely yellow and although I had no medical training I could see how sick she was.

The girl explained that her mother had given birth to a baby recently. The baby hadn't survived and now the mother was very sick too. I was baffled; I couldn't believe that so close to where I grew up people were living like that. I removed my hat, gloves and the jacket that I had on under my cape and gave them to the child telling her that I would be back in one hour. I turned the car around and went back home.

Thankfully, nobody was home, so I went to the storage space and grabbed some blankets and comforters and took them to my car. Then I dragged half a sack of rice to the car (around fifty pounds), of which Dad used to buy a few for our yearly consumption. I came back and took a portable kerosene heater and fitted that in the little car too. The last thing that I had to get was some cooking oil which again we had plenty of in our house.

I drove back to that road and found the girl standing at the corner of the highway waiting for me. Immediately, as I pulled over and descended from the car, I saw four young boys coming from nowhere, to help carry the stuff to the valley where they were living. After leaving them I was crying in my car as I drove along, thinking:
"Why haven't they got better living conditions? How many more unfortunate people in our country are living like these people?"
I knew well, what I had just done was nothing compared to what was needed to be done. I knew I had just satisfied myself by putting a small bandage on a huge bleeding wound...

After that, I tried to read and listen more to learn about the problems we had in Iran. It was not an easy task when the whole media was controlled by the government. I learned some and I used my sense of logic to guess some more. I realized that what I had seen was probably the best living condition compared to what was happening all around my country. I realized that those people were able to be in Tehran and close to a highway so there must have been thousands or millions in villages and street corners of small cities all around the country who didn't even have what those people were able to gather for themselves.

So, yes...there was a variety of pictures of Iran, as in many countries and they weren't all rich colorful portraits. They weren't all dingy poverty-stricken, religiously down-trodden portraits either. That is the point that I'd like the people of the West to fully understand. My background was stably rooted in well-off, "good" foundations and I wasn't alone.

At a wedding around 1971 in Tehran. From the left, it's me, our mom, my sister and our brother.

When I came to the US people would ask me: "What was the biggest shock for you? The clothing? The way we dress?" Not at all! I've always dressed like this, since I was a child. It was only after the revolution that people were forced to dress like that, the way you see in the news now. You may be shocked to hear that I wore bikinis and my mother wore bathing suits too. I have a photo of her in a bathing suit, taken about seventy years ago. Speaking of photos, I'd like to share some more photos with you here so that you can see for yourself what Iranian clothing habits were like in the life before the Ayatollah:

My parents' wedding c. 1949, Tehran

Mom's mom, Iran c. 1960

Mom at a formal party c. 1960 (she is the third one from the right).

A family wedding back in the early 1970's. My mom is the second one from the left.

1986, Tehran. I wanted to follow my mother's tradition and have a nice family picture with my children.

And in contrast – a photo to send to the prison, for Polad (the photo was denied).

The truth be known, I wasn't shocked by anything when I arrived in the US. I was surprised at how people dressed down when they went out, in casual clothing like sweatshirts and jogging pants. In Iran, the big difference between the classes was made evident by the clothing. We dressed like we had literally stepped out of a magazine.

On an aside note, another surprise for me was the number of overweight people. (I have to say that I gradually joined them through the years of living here too!) Another unfamiliar ground for me was dating! I'd never dated. I'd had a boyfriend for five years and no sex. When I think back, dating was horrendous for me. I was absolutely clueless as to the rules of the game.

Other than these exceptions there weren't shocking differences for me. So, you see, it's important for me to break the ignorance in the West when it comes to Iran and her people. So many people see us as deprived people coming to live in the US as if we are suddenly their equals. It's sad but amusing at the same time to still be asked, thirty odd years later, if we had TV. It's irritating when people react to wedding photos with such an air of shock: "You're dressed just like us!" Yes, we were and believe me when I say that that wasn't unusual.

Let's go back to February 1979 for a brief moment to illustrate one of the "whys" for this book.

"This is the voice of the revolution of the Iranian people!" announces Jamshid Adili on the radio after a few seconds of broadcasting silence, as the retreating tanks reached Shemiran Avenue. Again, he echoed: "This is the voice of the revolution of the Iranian people!" after which followed the broadcasting of Banan singing the anthem "Ey Iran" across the planet...

This was a very emotional moment for Iran and her people. Indeed, the broadcaster was on the verge of tears. This was a profound statement with such meaning, which ironically transmuted into the small voice, but extreme portion of the Iranian people. In reality, the Iran that the people had been fighting for didn't materialize. The true voice of the Iranian people was strangled... Our dreams were crushed by the new regime.

A culturally rich and colorful nation was transmuted into a grey country full of frightened people under the control of a small number of fundamentalist extremists who deceived their way into power. In their naivety and ideals of a unified nation, the revolutionists had become trapped. Celebration soon transformed into complete astonishment, incomprehension and loss. The people of Iran had been fully deceived. There is no other term for it. For me, the revolution was not a success because the whole population could not support that revolution any longer. In fact, only a small proportion of the population now supported the revolution! Now that the blinkers had been taken away, the revolution had taken the people of Iran from one dictatorship to another. Deception soon lay heavy on our chests.

I found some quotes from Ayatollah Khomeini which are strikingly in contrast with the reality in Iran. It's interesting to see his words before and after the revolution, illustrating the stark difference between what he was saying before the Islamic Republic and what he said afterwards and what happened in the country with imprisonments, executions etc.-- how he turned on everybody but the fundamentalist extremists.

Permit me to share some Ayatollah quotes[1] showing how his promises, before the Islamic Republic came into place, were so different to the reality that hit with a hard, bloody and even deathly clout...

Just look at what he was saying before the Islamic Regime took over and the contrasting statements afterwards, and not only his words but the actions that took place, that are still taking place:

"After the Shah's departure from Iran, I will not become a president nor accept any other leadership role. Just like before, I limit my activities only to guiding and directing the people." -Ayatollah Khomeini (in an interview with Le Monde newspaper, Paris, January 9, 1979).

So, who was it in the leadership role then? Who was it who came like a thief in the night and stole the revolution from under the feet of all the other revolutionists united in their chant of "Down with the Shah"? Who was it that took Iran backwards and oppressed the people, in many ways worse than the Shah. This is just one among a number of statements made by Khomeini where he denies the leadership role of himself and the clergy, and notice the date; it was so close to the revolution finale.

In an interview with Reuters news agency, October, 1978, Khomeini stated:

"In Islamic Iran the clergy themselves will not govern but only observe and support the government's leaders. The government of the country at all levels will be observed, evaluated, and publicly criticized."

In reality the clergy were governing and no criticism of them was tolerated, as was revealed by Khomeini himself when he spoke in a meeting with the Islamic Parliament in Tehran, May, 1981:

"This nation exists and clerics exist too. You all must know that in every place in this country only clerics can get the job done. Don't show so much prejudice that you want to put the clerics aside. What have you done for your country in all these years that now you're saying clerics should not be in charge? Appreciate these clerics..."

---

[1] Dr. Jalal Matini "The Most Truthful Individual in Recent History" – Iranshenasi Journal (Vol. XIV, No. 4, 2003)

In Paris, in October 1978, in an interview with France Press news agency Ayatollah Khomeini is quoted as saying: *"The Islamic regime does not have oppression."* Really? So, what has been happening over all these years, if not oppression? (Yes, dear reader; I'm angry at any controlling system on people. I'm a woman too.) Iranian women realized, within less than a month after the revolution, what oppression was, at the order of this man who had stated the contrary. Women soon realized that they were the victims of an anti-woman regime.

They were the first to be targeted even though Khomeini had said that it would not be so:

"These words that you have heard regarding women in the future Islamic government are all hostile propaganda. In the Islamic Republic women have complete freedom, in their education, in everything that they do, just as men are free in everything."

(In November 1978 during an interview with German reporters in Paris).

And:

"Women are free in the Islamic Republic in the selection of their activities and their future and their clothing."

(In an interview with The Guardian newspaper at a similar time).

Well, what a cauldron of lies we have here related to all people mentioned. Who was it spouting propaganda? Who was it lying? Even a man, who is apparently worth twice a woman, doesn't have complete freedom. Look at education. It wasn't long before the universities were shut down during armed seizures.

For three days, we had a truly free country! We all remember those three free days. The Shah was out, Khomeini hadn't announced anything yet. Television and radio weren't controlled…yet. They said whatever they wanted. "We are free… You can have your ideology as long as you don't hurt anyone… There are going to be representatives of all the groups… The country will be free…" After three days it all shut down. Television and radio started going totally Muslim. "Women have to cover their hair," was broadcast on the radio. We were looking at each other in astonishment. "What?" Then we realized that we had kicked out one dictator for another. Seventy thousand were killed in the streets of Iran for Khomeini to come in and oppress the Iranian people.

What were Khomeini's words about religion? During an interview with an Austrian reporter in November 1978 he claimed:

"In the Islamic Republic the rights of the religious minorities are respectfully regarded."

Ah. So why were people like my beloved Aunty Nour and her husband imprisoned, tortured and executed because they refused to give up their Baha'i faith? The worm turned!

"My proposal for establishing an Islamic government does not mean a return to the past. I am strongly for civilization and progress" were the words of Ayatollah Khomeini during a pre-revolution interview in Paris, January 11, 1979. Yet when speaking at the University of Science and Industry in Qom, August 1981, the Khomeini worm had definitely turned to:

"We would like to have a university in the service of our own nation, not a university whose slogan is that we want a civilized and modern Iran, which wants to move toward a great civilization..."

He didn't even choke on his words.

Did a true word ever come out of his mouth before the revolution? I rest my case dear reader. I could go on, but panic not! I will leave my anger and the other quotes aside and after this interlude, will now continue with my story...

I entitled this work "Numb" for a reason. That was my state, my feeling (or non-feeling in this case), on the night when I became aware that my revolutionist husband, Polad had disappeared, had been taken... In planning the writing of my memoir, I've come to realize that numbness wasn't a product of that one night alone. It seems like I had been already preparing for that numbness, to enable me to get through... but I lost something deep within my soul in exchange for becoming numb. Perhaps the writing of the memoir will enable me to retrieve that something.

I had to become numb to shield myself. It was as if everything was being taken away from me. My lovely aunt, Nour was imprisoned and eventually executed for being of the Baha'i religion. Polad didn't want me to mourn for Aunty Nour, saying that she was illogical; all she had to do was state that she was Muslim. Mom and my sister left Iran to start a new life. Dad had treated Mom badly and left her for another woman. I didn't have friends. Polad was my only family, my only rock to lean against, but he didn't have time for me. I couldn't continue with these feelings of abandonment without some kind of armor for both strength and protection.

I was numb for some time before, because I was not being permitted to be my true self. I was receiving limiting pressure from various angles (but mostly from my husband) and my way of not only protecting myself but also going forward was to become numb. My life was being spent in preparation for this ultimate numbness on that fateful night. I was giving but not receiving. It seems as if I was feeling undeserving. Maybe that paradigm dictated my choice of marriage partner to me; was that why I married someone who didn't treat me well?

Numbness, as my shield, gave me a feeling of being settled, sheltered. If I didn't feel anything much, then no one could hurt me anymore.

In contrast to that, once my first child came along, I suddenly had a baby giving me oceans of love. Not only that, Amir needed me; I gave him all the love and attention and in that giving, I felt fulfilled. Very soon, my fragile daughter, Maral was born. I had been handed two helpless creatures that depended upon me, who needed me to be strong. To accomplish my purpose I had got to be strong. So that numbness was broken down when it came to my children. I was running on two levels, as it were, immersed in such a contrast of feelings.

Outside the realm of loving connection with my children, the numbness was my cocoon, or my chrysalis preparing me for my transmutation into the butterfly, which would take place as from that October evening in 1983.

All those months and even years of fighting with Polad had stopped. In the last two years I had refused to get into a fight. I stopped feeling sorry for myself. I stopped feeling love for Polad. I stopped being hurt. Outside the realm of my babies, I was in automatic functioning mode. On the night when Polad came home and told me we had to go to friends, I just packed a suitcase with no feeling at all. I left our home with a fifteen day old daughter and less than two year old son. From that moment on, our lives would change dramatically.

I will be sharing some childhood memories with you too, my reason being that I want it to be evident to you how we were an ordinary family, not so very different from a Western quite well-off family. I was not a poor little starving young woman who escaped to the US from a poverty-stricken life… In sharing some of my background and describing some of the main influencing characters who have roles in my memoir story, I hope to enlighten you, if you have a picture of me riding around on a camel in Iran, and then coming to the US and benefitting from the delights of a developed country and culture. I already was used to these delights!

The aim of this memoir is to relate the story, but also to give you an insight into my thoughts and reasoning behind the writing and sharing of it. I've decided to finish the prologue with some excerpts from my diary at the time, so that you can feel my state during this period and experience my pain and anger in all perspectives. This ongoing pain and anger has shown itself in various intensities and guises from then until now. Maybe this sharing with you will prove to be a release for me. Thank you dear reader for being my therapist!

Former revolutionaries in the late 1970s who had been working together in various factions, along with the religious Muslim group, had now become enemies of the new republic which they had fought to bring about – mistakenly, as it turned out. I hadn't understood the danger or reality of this situation. Polad had continued to resist.

Thursday April 26, 1984

This is the first time this year that I am writing in this book. I have repeatedly talked about destiny's unfair games during the last 14 years, on these pages, yet this time the pain is greater than any of my previous sorrows that I have ever mentioned in this book. Our sun was stolen from us. My husband, my Polad was taken away from his children. It has been 6 months that we haven't seen him with any knowledge about his whereabouts. Little Amir is sitting behind our apartment door waiting for his "Baba" (dad) to come home with Coke and ice cream. He sleeps on the floor waiting for him.

Inside my heart I know that he is still alive. I can feel it. He is somewhere and is thinking about his children. The last night that I saw him was November 12th 1983 when our daughter, Maral was 4 weeks old. My father arrived from visiting my Mom and family 20 days ago. It is helping my little boy Amir a lot to have his Papa around but Maral knows nothing of what is going on. She is sitting in her walker and making noises. Hey, dear Polad, I know your red-hot heart is craving to see and hold your children. Ah my dear, come home soon, come home soon before I have to explain your absence to our children. NuRuz (Iranian New Year in March) was quiet and lonely. I didn't do anything special. I didn't have money for new clothing for the kids and no desire to decorate.

Saturday June 16, 1984

We have been able to visit Polad 3 times so far -- 3 x 10 minutes through the thick glass with a phone. My life is hard; not financially, but my soul and nerves are extremely shut down. Something is being destroyed inside me, I don't have the strength that I had a few months ago any more. Why am I melting from inside? I feel old; I feel that I have aged 10 or 20 years during the past few months. I feel ill; I know I am not well. God, what will happen if I get so sick that I cannot protect my kids? Something is burning inside me. I cannot talk to anybody about the way I feel inside. People should not see my weakness. They will attack and hurt us if they know I am melting from inside. I must be strong, must play it like a soldier. I know I can, I know I can, I MUST. Maral is 8 months old now with no teeth and doesn't sit up yet. Something must be wrong; Amir had teeth at 5 months and sat at 6 months. It must be my fault. I didn't eat well; I didn't give enough calcium to my baby while she was inside my belly counting on me to protect her. Amir is doing much better. He is bonding with my father and started listening to me again. He talks so cute and moves his arms up and down with lots of expression on his cute little face with those big black eyes. Ah my son, my buddy I will teach you to love the fall in Tehran. I will teach you the love of rain and the love of September as it has been so precious to me all my life.

August 23rd, 1984

My beloved autumn is coming. September is around the corner. Fall is coming with its sad weather and all that it has to say. I was born in the fall. I was married in the fall. My husband was taken from us in the fall. I gave birth to two beautiful children in the fall. I know I will die on a beautiful yellow and orange fall day and leaves will be blowing around as my family is gathering around my graveside to say their goodbyes.

Jan 30th, 1985

They say he will come home late, very late many years later. It can't be; it can't be... It must be a lie... I wish I was dead the day before becoming a mother. How can I explain to my son that he will be growing up without his father? See what you did Polad? See what you did to me, to our kids and yourself... Ahhh I do wish I was dead. I wish I could sit in a corner and just die.., Who can I talk to? Nobody... I am that lonely unfortunate person who has not one star in seven skies. I am not feeling well... I have been feeling very ill for a year... the cough that comes out of my guts, the sores on my hands, the rush to get to the toilet and accidents when I am not fast enough... I feel old...very old.

On that sad, dark note let's exit the prologue and enter my memories of that period in my life and how I came out the other side as a butterfly with new wings, and able to share with you and bring some of the true Iran to you for the sake of standing up for love and justice... Discover how I was forced to leave Iran and participate in the journey of finding myself and making a new life for my children. Through it all the essence of my soul remained untouched. My soul carried me through.

Chapter One

"I think they got him."
Numb is Numb, is My Sword and Shield.

I was waiting…
It was almost 2.30 a.m. and I couldn't sleep. Every sound from the street behind the house was making me jump, thinking that Polad was back. How hot and uncomfortable it was in that little basement apartment. There had been a lot of people gathered there for such a small space. I can remember there had been some talking and laughing going on around me, but I really don't recall much of those twenty-four hours. They remain as a fog.

I had realized that the atmosphere was not normal when we arrived there. Soon after, some other friends of Polad showed up too. The place was far too small for all of us. Besides, I knew that Polad and his buddies wouldn't gather in one place unless it was absolutely necessary. It was not a comfortable situation for any one of us.

The apartment belonged to Polad's friends, Nader and Susan, a young couple with a little daughter. It consisted of one room which had become two rooms with the drapes drawn across the center. The back room, with mattresses on the floor was providing bedroom space for the females – Susan, her daughter and her mother, along with me and my two children. I wasn't comfortable with my two babies and I'm sure Susan didn't like all of us in her little apartment either. Polad's friends where coming and going quietly. On top of all that Susan's mother was also staying there.

I can't recall if it was that very night or the next day when Polad left that house never to return. All I remember is the night passing from 10 to 11, from 12 to 1 a.m. and all the way through 4 and 5 a.m. and he failed to come through that door. Those hours slowly and torturously passing, one after another will remain with me forever.

If I had been home I would have taken a shower or changed my clothing for something more comfortable, but I couldn't do that. I hated having to go through the hours of the day and night fully dressed. I could not believe how hot that little place was although it didn't seem to bother anybody else! I was quiet, sitting in the corner, trying to be invisible to those who probably knew very well what was happening to me and my children.

I was still sitting in the front room, still waiting… looking up, watching the rain hitting the windows above my head on road level. Water splashed from the passing cars with a pschoo. My babies were asleep and there was no sound in the apartment. The only noise was coming from the street.

I sat waiting, waiting… not really aware of the room around me. Were there paintings on the walls? Nader and Susan were both artists, graduated from the University of Tehran. You'd expect there to be paintings wouldn't you? I can't tell you.

I sat waiting, waiting, not sure why Polad was late. I was still expecting him back soon. Nader entered the room, as quiet as a cat. His pale face and terrified but sorrowful expression did nothing to calm my anxiety! With an apologetic air he mumbled: "I think they got him." I'd known in my heart that he wasn't coming back that night, but the words quietly slipping between Nader's lips made it as real and lonely as I'd ever felt in my life.

I was staring at Nader's mouth hoping that there would be something more that he hadn't told me yet. Something around the lines of: "….but we know where he is" or "We know some-one who can give us more information about his situation," but there was nothing else left for him to say. I felt numb. I was unable to think. I just knew that the children would wake up soon and they would need food, diapers and a safe place. That moment has stayed in my mind as fresh as this morning's sound of my alarm clock. I felt inert and hard of hearing. I leaned forward very close to Nader trying to hear him well as his voice was not reaching me. I felt very hot; sweat began running down my forehead and blurring my eyes, and yet my hands felt extremely cold.

I'd been attempting to convince myself that he'd be back, that he wasn't gone, gone… Nader continued speaking. We were standing just three feet from each other, but I couldn't hear him anymore. I'd gone completely deaf, it seemed. After his dramatic statement, my head became filled with a potion of thoughts:
Where was Polad?
Where has he been?
Was he shot?
Was there a street fight?

There was a little "It serves him right" in the mix too! I don't deny it. Yes, I was angry with him, angry at the abandonment, angry for my children. In that moment it wasn't about me; my concerns were oriented toward my children. I wasn't thinking "Oh, what am I going to do? My world's caving in, tumbling down on me." Funnily enough, I had a matter of fact reaction: "Okay, that's happened. What about the kids? I've no money to buy formula. I'm not breast feeding well due to the stress…"

Having the children actually saved my life. Having the children forced me to hold on to my sense of responsibility. "I brought these two little human beings into the world and I'm responsible for them now, on my own." If it hadn't been for my children I would probably have been destroyed – committed suicide…

The night we left to go to Nader's, we'd had an argument. I'd said: "You go; you're the one doing these political actions. They don't have anything against me." He told me that I didn't understand – "They have everything against you! Your father was working for Shah. You are a registered Baha'i regardless of whether you are religiously active or not. Your aunt was executed for being Baha'i. You are married to a very active socialist. They'll come to get you to make me talk."

I quickly ironed a blue and white stripe shirt for him; I wanted him to look good. I'm chuckling at the thought of it. Why did I do that? I guess I did love him. I was angry with him. Then I quietly got into the car with the children and we made our 'escape' to Nader's apartment.

So, here I was standing in front of Nader, unable to hear his words, actually unable to feel. I felt nothing. I felt no anger, no sorrow, no tears, no happiness, no hunger. I felt nothing. I knew that I had to shut everything down other than making sure the children were alright. My thoughts were for my children. What am I going to feed the kids when they wake up? Is there any food in the house for Amir? As I was under so much pressure my milk had almost dried up. Would I be able to nurse Maral? I didn't have money to buy formula. These were my thoughts at that moment; they weren't for me, how I felt, my marriage… No, my only thoughts were for my children.

Chapter Two
Polad

How did we come to this? Polad and I met back in the fall of 1973 in a Baha'i youth gathering program in Tehran. At the time, I was 17 and he was 19 years old. I was in my last year of high school and he had been graduated the year before. My family was financially well to do and he was from a hard working one. Both families were well educated, but there was a large gap in social status.

He was a very good-looking young man with large black eyes, slightly pulled up at the outer sides. Later on I found out that his father's side of the family was from Kurdistan and he had all the features that went with that ancestry. The thunder like voice, dark large eyes, short nose and the body structure of a weight lifter were all there to prove it. Like most Iranian men, he was not tall but built beautifully masculine. His name meant steel in Kurdish, what a great name for someone with his personality. I remember the day he called our house; the first time that I heard his voice is still very fresh in my mind.

I was 17 years old and after finishing the twelve year Baha'i school stopped attending any Baha'i youth programs. Due to coming from a mixed religion family, I wasn't very comfortable with Baha'i rules both written and unwritten ones. I liked my makeup and tight jeans and many of those girls weren't that way. They were more apt to act in a classic lady behavior with clothing that their mom or older sister would wear.

Polad was a very determined young man who had a heart of gold. He would literally take the shirt off his back and offer it to someone who seemed to need it more than him. I'm not exaggerating in saying that not only was he well loved by people but he was almost worshipped by some. Money never had much of a meaning to him, so he wouldn't handle it as responsibly as perhaps he should have. He could easily part with what he had, so he really couldn't understand others' reactions regarding the concept of "their money" versus "someone else's money". If he had $10 and someone would have asked for it, he would definitely give it all to that friend without thinking about his own needs, such as food that night or a bus ticket to get home.

When Polad and I were together for years before getting married I realized that the big gap between our families' social status was far more serious than we both gave any thoughts to. My father, who had a sensitive job in the government at the time, didn't care for Polad, his family or his line of thinking. My mother, on the other hand, who was always a dreamer, didn't think of anything but how good-looking Polad was and how kind he was towards her.

Meeting Polad – The Fall of 1973

I was home; our phone rang and a man with this beautiful thunder-like voice asked to speak with Miss Azita. I confirmed that I was the person he was asking for, so he introduced himself and said that he was a member of the "Tehran Baha'i Youth" and would like to invite me to that Thursday night's youth gathering. I tried to come up with some excuses but he wouldn't take "no" for an answer! Finally, he suggested picking me up that afternoon and walking me to the gathering. Well, at that point I had no way of getting out of it so I agreed.

The doorbell rang and there he was standing there as handsome as I ever imagined him to be. He had a beautiful smile and very bright large dark eyes. It started there and finally I became a member of the Baha'i youth group too. I had had twelve years of Baha'i school education and had been involved with the Baha'i Teens group a year before meeting him. Somehow, I didn't feel that I belonged with the other boys and girls and had separated myself.

Around the summer of 1972, I felt very comfortable with a very short haircut, black eye shadow, very narrow eyebrows, lots of mascara, jeans and my father's shirts and sweaters that would come down to just above my knees. That all changed too after meeting Polad.

Polad was from a very religious Baha'i family. During our five years of friendship he gradually changed his outlook towards being a Baha'i and became closer and closer to the socialism ideology. The Baha'i religion allows boys and girls to be in contact, go to school together and have friendship. Education is a very important element of this religion and there is absolute equality between men and women.

We were taught to believe in many principles in life that seem to be simple but deeply important. We were told that you must not touch something that doesn't belong to you, without permission, even if it belongs to your best friend. We were told that there is no hell or heaven on the other side, but only our souls that would be close to God like being in Heaven, or suffering from being away from him like being in hell. Thus, there are a lot of differences between Baha'i and Islamic beliefs and we all knew the rumors that the Muslim leaders had spread around about Baha'ism.

The freedom of females was the most bothersome matter for Muslim leaders. Consequently, the first accusation was that sexual relationships between siblings were allowed among Baha'i families. The second full blown accusation which is still going strong was that "Baha'ism is not a religion; it is a political charade invented by the English Government back in the nineteenth century". All of this was because Muslim leaders could not bring themselves to believe that there could be other religions as well as theirs! In case you would like to read more about this matter, I suggest you Google the word Baha'i to get some more information.

Polad and I used to go for very long walks together during the first few months of our relationship. Farah Park, also known as Keshavarz Park, was one of the places that we could walk and talk in for hours. He had no money for fancy entertainment and I wasn't much interested in going to the disco or cafés anymore! Yes, I actually had done all of that with my previous boyfriends, and I knew well not to mention any of those experiences to Polad.

During all of those hand in hand walks we talked about everything from the meaning of life to philosophy, nature and even martial arts! For the longest time he never made any direct comment about what exactly was going on in Iran or what could be the solution or anything along those lines. I remember, after a year or so he talked about South American countries, especially Pinochet and his crimes in Chile. Wow, these were totally new subjects for me to think about. Where I came from; the world was fine and people were nice and more or less everybody had what they needed.

After a year or two, Polad grew out of the Baha'i gatherings and so did I. He didn't bad mouth the religion, but he was convinced that he would be more useful to his society by politically educating himself. That's what he did.

It was known to my family and friends that I had a boyfriend. I didn't take him to our family gatherings or insist for him to take me to his, but we were together as much as we could be. The love between us was intense and our fights were even more so.

To me it was clear that I should and would marry him and, since I had never openly had a boyfriend before, my family was under the same impression. None of us was a "player" and both families knew we were inseparable so nobody gave us any grief about our relationship. The love we felt at that age was extremely intense. I couldn't eat and sleeping wasn't easy either. Just like in some romantic comedy movies, I could see his face on everybody, even on the billboards! His voice was the remedy for all my pains and I wished I could carry around a recording of him just talking about daily subjects.

If I was sick I would walk and take a cab to go to the other side of Tehran just to be with him. I would go there to sleep in his bed even if he wasn't home. I would lie down in his bed looking at what he would look at every time he was in bed. His books on the shelf and the bottle of sea water that he had asked me to bring him as a souvenir from our family trip to the Caspian Sea shore a while back. It was a pretty liquor bottle that I filled up with some soft sand and sea water and held in my hands during the four hour car ride from the Caspian Sea to Tehran as my father drove us back home. You could see some moving little sea creatures and some silver sand at the bottom of that bottle which made it look so beautiful.

The bedding had his body aroma and I would go to sleep in no time until he would come back from classes or work. I was in love with him as I had never felt before in my life. It was beautiful, harsh, soft, happy and sad all at the same time…

After maybe six or eight months of being with Polad, I decided to throw a party at our house. As our parents used to travel to our shore house every now and then, it wasn't hard to find a day that we could have the house to ourselves. My sister and I were so excited, and I decided to make the formal living room look like a disco. We had this large chandelier with twelve 100 W light-bulbs in our formal living room. I changed six of them with red and the other six with blue colored light bulbs. We had so much fun that night with dancing, talking and having tasty sandwiches. Everybody left around 11 p.m. and I totally forgot about the light bulbs.

A few days later my dad came home with two or three important men, dressed in black suits, ties and even hats. They walked in and my dad flipped the switch; BAM (!!!!) The room was half red and half blue! I saw the look on my dad's face and knew that I had to get out of there really fast. I saw him pressing his lips together, trying so hard not to call me names in front of his important guests. As he walked to the kitchen to get the step ladder I was out of the house and half way to the main intersection.

Years passed; Polad and I both entered colleges after high school. My college was about fifteen miles outside of the city of Tehran and he attended the Drama College of the University of Tehran. Our relationship was a combination of love and hatred. Numerous fights, name callings and accusations were a part of our daily routine.

After entering college I began to realize that I was kind of attractive and I could probably do better than Polad, but my heart was with him and nothing, even his ridiculous tantrums, could change that. At that time my mother started getting more serious about our relationship and tried to talk to me, but I didn't give her enough time or attention to be the mother that I needed so badly at that time. Looking back now I know that I just needed to get out of my parents' house, and marrying Polad was the easiest and fastest way to accomplish that.

During the time we were going out together Polad's family moved out of the city and bought a beautiful large house in the suburb. As Polad was a college student in Tehran he remained in their old apartment. He was working and going to university at the same time to be able to have his financial independence and continue his education. I was still living at home and would go to see him as soon as I didn't have a class or had got off classes a bit early.

I needed to be around him so badly that I would forget how miserable we could get after each fight. If I woke up sick with the flu or something like that I would go to Polad's apartment just to sleep in his bed -- that's all -- and I would feel better if I was close to him. One summer night I woke up around 3 a.m. and walked to the balcony via the French window in my room. I stood there holding the railing and just couldn't go back to bed for ten or fifteen minutes. The next day, when I saw Polad, he asked if I had slept well, I told him that I had, but I had woken up in the middle of the night and walked to the balcony, for no apparent reason. He smiled and asked if it was around 3 a.m. When I told him that it was and asked him why he had asked, he said: "Because I was calling you in my head."

Chapter Three

Family and Background Influences Childhood Memories

The house felt different. My mother was talking on the phone as my dad came home with lots of groceries. His scoffer was helping him carry everything inside. Mom was very busy in the kitchen that day. People were cleaning our house and washing the large front porch, moving the large plant pots around. A dining room table was carried from our normal living room outside onto the porch. One of our old butlers arrived around 4 p.m. to help my mom.

We, the children, were fed and told to go upstairs around 8 p.m. and we knew we weren't allowed to come down. My dad had a "guy's party" that night. Men, all dressed in black suits, ties and hats came over for drinks and dinner. No background music, just their voices could be heard. Mom was in the kitchen and our old butler was taking the trays to the formal living room to serve the guests.

We could sometimes be a little mischievous, as all children can. On this occasion, somehow, my sister and I snuck into the kitchen, poured soda into those pretty glasses and pretended to be drinking alcohol! We were laughing and having so much fun! Back then you needed a bottle opener to open a soda bottle, and they used to hide it from us. We soon learned to grab a large nail and a hammer to make a hole in the top and drink the soda! Later on, our brother showed us how to use the door knob holes to do that! My dad would be so angry with us because he couldn't close any downstairs doors properly anymore.

My parents back in 1951 when expecting their first child (my brother); they were happy and in love back then.

I was born in 1956 in an upper middle class family in Tehran. My parents were both working in education related jobs. Mom told us how our parents met. My dad was a 26 year old tall, dark and handsome school principal when my 21 year old mother became a teacher at the same school. My dad was from a very traditional Muslim family, but my mother was Baha'i, a member of the minority religious group in Iran. Their love story was a sweet one with many ups and downs until they were able to convince the two very different families to agree to their marriage.

Another family picture in Tehran, before my sister was born.

Thus they commenced their lives together and soon my father climbed the promotion ladder and was given the position of "General Chief of Education" for the State of Tehran. All of the education system from elementary to high schools, throughout the State of Tehran were under his control. My mother kept her teaching job as a part time 'hobby' to have some spending money of her own.

I have a brother who is three years older and a sister who is almost four years younger than me. As for our religious backgrounds, our parents agreed that we would receive both Islamic and Baha'i instruction so that we would decide for ourselves which one we would like to join as adults. All three of us were pulled more towards being Baha'i and all of us went through the confirmation ceremony at age 15. I don't think my father liked that, but he never openly showed his disappointment over this matter.

My parents' love story ended about ten years into their marriage. My father, who felt separated from his children due to having different religious and cultural beliefs, fell in love with another woman. He became distanced from our mother and very quiet with all of us at home. He would hardly smile any more. Nothing changed on the surface; he would come home every night and he would take us on vacation to his shore house in North Iran during summer time. Their marriage would continue for many years to come simply because my mother couldn't bring herself to leave him. Now that I look back I see that our home was so cold and empty. I just wanted to get out of there regardless of how I did it.

We had a normal family life when I was a small child. I remember my dad laughing and playing with us. I remember he used to lie on his back, put his big feet on my belly, grab my hands and fly me up and down and make crowing sounds! I loved sleeping on my dad's big tummy and he didn't mind it at all. I must have been very small because my whole body, including my feet would cover his chest and stomach only.

Back then the family used to have "game nights". My mom's sisters and my grandmother used to live down the street from us. Once a week, we would walk to my aunt's house and the brother in-laws would play cards or Backgammon. Sometimes one of the wives would play with them, but mostly it was a guy's thing. The funniest thing was hearing these big guys screaming at each other and then ending their bickering with loud laughter and another round of hot tea. Unfortunately for all of us, those days didn't last long…

Everything vanished and turned to ashes in our house after my father fell in love with another woman. Our home turned to a quiet and cold place with us family members just coming and going like mechanical dolls. I still believe that my parents should have divorced, but they didn't. We all lived a lie with a happy family appearance for outsiders. Mom lived in denial, believing that someday he would come back to her. Dad lived a double life to keep matters looking normal.

My father climbed the promotion ladder and was given the position of "General Chief of Education" for the State of Tehran. He was a hard working believer of that regime.

There are four seasons in Tehran and when I was a child we used to get a lot of snow during the three winter months. Men used to walk in the streets with wooden snow shovels on their shoulders loudly announcing their service of shoveling the snow for some remuneration. My mother always invited these guys inside, so they could shovel the snow from our flat roof.

As a child, I always found it difficult to see these young men, without enough clothing and without gloves doing such hard work for so little money. They had to shovel the flat roof and throw the snow, one shovel at a time, into the yard. They had to launch it out far enough so that it wouldn't land on the second floor balcony, which went from one side of the house all the way to the other. Then, they had to come back into the yard and clear a walkway path from the first floor porch to the yard door.

There would be a very high amount of snow on both sides of the pathway which would become our North-Pole playground! During the days when school was closed due to heavy snow, my brother and I used to get on our hands and knees and make a few tunnels around the yard and move through them. My sister was the youngest so she would follow us into the tunnels, get cold and wet and cry. Mom would get mad at us and tell us to stay inside. So we really didn't want our little sister following us or playing with us…but sometimes we had no other choice.

My brother and I, Tehran

It was the summer of 1966 and my brother and I were playing on our long, wide front porch. We had one pair of skates that we were supposed to share. As you may remember, those skates were made of metal with a key that you could use to change the size to fit different shoe sizes. We would wear one each and use the other foot to roll up and down the porch. My brother, however wasn't very happy with this sharing arrangement and wanted so badly to skate with both feet, as we had seen on the American channel of our television. He fixed both skates to his size and hid the key from me! He was skating up and down the porch, trying to keep his balance and I was chasing him and trying to push him into the wall… It didn't end well at all, and Mom had to interfere before my brother would hurt me.

We had a very small pool in our yard with a fountain in the middle. It was normal for all Iranian yards to have one; the water was used for watering the plants and it was pleasant for sitting around during summer evenings, enjoying the relaxing sound of the fountain water splashing. Almost all Iranian children would play in these little pools to cool off on summer days. I remember my mother recounted stories from her childhood when they all played in their pool in the yard, which was apparently big enough to swim in.

One hot summer day, as my brother and I were splashing and playing in the water he swam under my feet and made me jump up and land on my forehead at the side of the pool! Poor Mom had to take a screaming Azita, with blood running down her face to the hospital to get stitches! My brother always maintained a very quiet air, but was quite a handful beneath this outside appearance! As many brothers can be, of course.

My childhood is full of good memories. We and our cousins would play in our yard all summer long. We would create roads, intersections and bridges in our flower garden and move little cars and make automobile noises with our mouths! As we got a bit older we started to bury our old lunch boxes with some toys and notes in them for 'posterity' so that people, in the future, would find them! In order to remember the location, we would make up some rhymes that nobody, but us, would understand. We had a lamp post in the garden which had a small plate in front of it near the dirt for wiring purposes. The last lunch box buried was in front of that plate so the rhyme for us to remember was:

"Across the door, beneath floor, don't say more!" Oh, we had such fun!

Sometimes, in my mind, I travel all the way to Tehran and go to our house to dig out all those 'treasures' that we buried to see if they are still there and if the notes and pictures survived after over fifty years! Recently, I heard that our building was demolished and they built many apartments instead. Who knows, maybe the construction workers found those lunch boxes and had a good laugh.

Our television had a door with a lock. Our parents would lock the door and hide the key so we wouldn't watch television all evening and neglect our school homework. They used that key (or the hiding of it) for just about every punishment. One day when they opened the television door to let us watch I took a good look at that key. As soon as I could get into my parents' bedroom, I searched everywhere and grabbed any key that I could find from the drawers and closets. I brought them all to the television room and checked them one by one. The key to my mother's jewelry cabinet worked perfectly in the television door. I put it back and then used it on the television cabinet for years to come without telling anybody about it.

I always felt myself to be entangled in the middle child syndrome, even when I was too young to know such a subject existed. My brother was the 'boy' and the first born and my sister was the baby so I was the invisible one! My mother and I never developed any relationships and soon after I left home she became very close to my younger sister. I believe that my mother put herself between us children and our father, to protect us; thus none of us actually became close to him. That is not exactly true; I was close to my dad, at least closer than I ever was to my mother.

I am about 8 years old in this picture taken in our yard in Tehran.

    Somehow I always felt that I wasn't what she had expected. I believe she was disappointed that I wasn't as pretty and light skinned as she imagined I would be. I was a tiny little tom-boy with frizzy hair, dark skin and big brown eyes, who never acted like a 'little girl'. I think I was about 16 when I felt somewhat pretty. It was too late to start any relationship with Mom because I had emotionally separated myself from her when I was 13 or 14, after feeling that I couldn't lean on her as a mom.

    For me, she was this very beautiful girl who never grew up to be a woman. I could see that she wasn't logical and making decisions was always a very difficult task for her. What I couldn't see, at the time, was that she had lost her father when she was only 10 years old; not having a male role-model in her life had left serious scars in her soul and personality. Now, I realize that my mother loved my father as her father, her husband and her savior -- something that my father never came to understand.

I believe that my parents had a wonderful relationship and a happy family for the first ten years of their marriage. All of my memories of togetherness, playing with my dad, seeing him laughing, at home go way back to when I was very little.

Things really started changing at home when I was probably 13 or 14 years old. My brother would have been around 17 and my sister would have been around 10 years old. Nobody knows what happened, but our home became cold and loveless.

My father would come home after work around 3 p.m. My mother was a part time school teacher and was going to college for her degree in English language. She was also interested in Persian classical music, so she was taking singing class as well. Back then, we had someone come in to do the house work and my father was the one who had full responsibility for paying the bills, fix whatever needed repairing in the house and the weekly major food shopping at the big Tehran Bazar.

As the coldness shadowed our home my dad started going out of town for business. He would sometimes be away for weeks or months. He would come home, take care of what we needed and go back to the other state that he was transferred to. This was our routine for many years until the phone calls started. People would call our house and hang up. Then we started rushing to get the phone first so we could say a few nasty words to the silent caller.

My mother, me and my sister in "Mashhad", Iran. My dad was transferred there for almost two years and that was when we found out about the other woman. We are at a historic site in this picture.

Through all of that, my mother was absolutely clueless that her husband might have another woman. In hindsight, it seems very clear; the other woman was calling to talk to my dad and she would hang up the phone when someone else answered it. We started saying things to the unknown caller; therefore she retorted with nasty things to every one of us.

When my brother was 19 years old he got into a horrific motorcycle accident. He was ill for months; we almost lost him. When he was home during his recovery, he received phone calls where the caller called him retarded and crippled. Through all of those incidences my father would just come home to make sure we had whatever we needed and my mother was oblivious to what was going on.

Finally, one evening Dad, who was out of town, called home to talk to Mom. Their conversation finished and they hung up. Mom wanted to call him back to remind him of something; she started dialing the number but the line was busy. After many attempts, it seemed as if the connection was made, but before she could speak, she heard my father's voice talking to a woman in a very intimate way. Apparently, the woman was giggly and said to my dad:
"Yes, (laughingly) I told them that the woman on the other side of you was your wife, ha ha ha." My dad replied: "Okay dear, I just wanted to say goodnight. Go to bed now."

You can perhaps imagine what happened next. My mom screamed a few words into the phone receiver and nobody responded. She dialed the number again and my dad answered the phone and very calmly said;
"Yes, did you forget something?"
"Who was that woman? I heard you talking and…" shouted Mom.
"What woman? What are you talking about?" calmly interrupted my dad. After that night, my dad acted as if nothing had happened. He would come and go with a long face as he had done for the past two or three years.

Then people started seeing a woman in the car with my father. They spoke about him and "his wife" going to lunch at work. I was 19 years old when one morning I came out of my room to see my mother half-naked sitting on the bed, ordering my father to divorce HER. I just couldn't and still can't digest my mother's actions as a logical response to the crises in her marriage. I felt very sorry for my mom and hated her at the same time for being so naive and weak. She could at least have told him not to come home again. She could have said "If you love her, then go live with her," but instead she tortured herself for more than three decades waiting for him to come back to her.

I remember telling her to pack a suitcase for him and change the house lock. She would just change the subject or act as if the whole thing was just a bad joke. My sister was the person who was affected most by the situation. I escaped by getting married. My brother was sent to the US to continue his education and that left my sister with Mom at home, day in and day out, asking *if he was with her right at that moment* or trying to read the cards on his behalf to verify *if he was really in love with her or not*… Sad, very sad situation for a 15 year old girl to be in.

My sister and Mom developed this weird relationship where my sister became Mom's protector instead of Mom taking care of my sister. This relationship developed into an even stronger one years later as they moved to the US to live with my brother. What Mom, my brother and sister created in the US, for almost ten years, was *a family* – the family we had lost twenty years prior to their gathering together in the US. These three beings became very close, tightly nourishing each other's emotional needs for years, as a classic family.

Once, when I was a mom myself, I directly asked my dad about his decision to not divorce my mom when he fell out of love with her. His answer was:
"Daughter, how anyone can know that I tried to do the right thing for everybody." I replied:
"What do you mean the right thing? Mom was in her forties; she was still young and could have started a new life…" He looked at me and shook his head. My sister and I concluded in our adult lives that he simply sacrificed our mother so as to have us around. He must have known that in the case of divorce my mother would have left Iran with her children to come to live near her brother in the US. In Iran, children are always given to the father, but did he and that woman want to have three children in their love shack? I don't think so…

One day back in 1970, when I was 14 years old, I got off the school bus to walk home. A few young construction workers started pushing me around and making fun of my black uniform. I opened my big mouth and said a few none flattering words to them. As a result, they hit and pushed me to the ground. The business owners were standing at their store openings watching and laughing. I cried all the way home wondering what that was about. Why did those men behave that way? I didn't tell my parents; somehow I felt that it was my own fault.

Ironically, I was dressed in my Catholic School uniform when I was beaten by those men in the streets of Tehran.

A year later when I was walking home from Baha'i school which was always just half a day during the weekend, I was attacked by a young man who was about to rape me. I wasn't dressed provocatively as I was coming back from Baha'i school. I began screaming from the depth of my being and cursing him; he abandoned his attempt.

I didn't see what was happening back then, but a few years later I realized that society was changing and actually dividing. The gap between the upper and downtown residents in Tehran was becoming as wide as a valley. In my family, socializing with boys was not forbidden, but we were supposed to follow the rules. My Armenian friends had a teen life as open and as free as western teens and I knew some of them were sexually active. The majority of the population that was Muslim was growing more and more towards the traditional code and the rest of us were growing more towards western family rules.

I would like to talk about women in Iranian society or teen life back in the early seventies, but I have to admit that all I have to say would be from my side of the story and not a general overall idea about Iranian society in that era.

It seems that we were living in a very different part of Tehran. I may be wrong, but I think where we lived must have been some sort of tourist area since the early sixties to the end of the seventies. Our street and two other parallel ones had more non-Muslim residents than Muslims. I don't recall seeing one Mosque within a ten mile radius of our house, but there were three churches! The bakeries were both owned by Armenians. There was a night club and two bars within walking distance from our house.

There were also three restaurants that we could walk to within five to ten minutes: one Italian, one French and the other one was a famous Persian restaurant. We lived as in western societies. My mother and us girls had no problem going to the swimming pools and the beach on the Caspian coast, wearing bathing suits or even bikinis. My mother's family was the same, if not a bit more modern than us. I remember talking to some teen relatives who had spent the summer in Europe; they spoke about topless bathing on some beaches which wasn't an easily digested subject for me.

My dad, who was from a traditional Muslim family, never showed any dislike about us and our mom dressing like westerners either. Our classmates were just like us. Some of my dad's relatives, on the other hand, had very different lives. Dad's nieces had traditional lives. I'm sure that they never slipped in to a bathing suit and never walked out of the house without covering their hair. If there were that many differences in just one family, you can say that the whole society was similar, a mixture of different family values, religions, customs and traditions. Around the north of Tehran, where I grew up, life was beautiful.

My parents had me signed up in ballet classes since I was maybe 10 years old for five or six years. I used to take the city bus and go to my ballet class on my own with no problem or fear. Later on when I was 13 or 14, my sister and I would take the bus and go to a public swimming pool.

Here we are standing in the yard back in early 70's posing for mom who was taking the picture.

I remember when we started wearing miniskirts in Tehran. Yes, we all started wearing those awfully short skirts and the smock dresses that were in fashion at that time, and walk out in the streets as if we were living in Europe. But many attacks on women happened during that time and we knew not to go far from our uptown homes in those outfits. The next trend was looking like the famous model "Twiggy". I must have been around 16 (1971/1972) when I cut my hair very short and started wearing lots of black makeup round my eyes.

Boys and girls had no problem walking together or socializing openly, although there were problems in some families who didn't allow their daughters to do that. Some of those families were extremely open-minded about their daughters spending time with other girls. We weren't allowed to sleep over at anybody's house, boy or girl, but some of my girlfriends would spend the night over at each other's houses and have some half naked dance parties. Parents were okay with whatever they were doing behind closed doors as long as no boy was involved!

The general atmosphere appeared to start changing, even in my neighborhood, around 1971 or 1972.

Our upbringing was based on Baha'i methods spiced with some European open-minded theories thanks to Mom! I can easily claim that we were different from all the other children. We didn't have limited (or no) freedom as the Muslim girls did and we weren't raised as very religious Baha'i children either. Mom told us she had had a deal with Dad that when they became parents, the children would receive a Baha'i education. We did go to Baha'i Sunday school for twelve years.

In school, the non-Muslim pupils could ask to not attend the Islam Study classes, but we didn't do that. The Baha'i religion was never recognized by that government, so we would sit in those classes also as if we were Muslim. In many cases, the teacher knew who we were and would deliberately pick on us or insult our beliefs openly and there was nothing we could do but sit there and take the abuse.

I think I was 16 when my brother left Iran for the US to continue his college education and that was when I moved to his room. I loved my new bedroom; I had large French windows to the extended upstairs front porch which had a wide view of the neighborhood. I had a desk, a phone and a small kerosene heater in that room. I really didn't need to leave the room very often. I would come home from school and later on college, check the refrigerator and go straight upstairs to my room. On cold and snowy days I used to make tea or hot cocoa on the small kerosene heater. Thus, as a family, we didn't have much sharing happening in our daily lives. Everybody was by him or herself. I knew the house rules and I didn't do anything to cause problems for myself. As you can see, I didn't have many reasons to interact with family members unless I needed a ride to some place.

When I was 16 years old, Dad would drive me to the ice skating rink and drop me off around 6 p.m. to pick me up later around 9 pm. As soon as he had driven away I would jump into a cab and go to a disco, meet my friends or boyfriend, dance the night away, and come back to the ice-skating rink before 9 o'clock for Dad to pick me up! The door man at the Ice-Skating rink didn't like the idea at all and one day he told Dad that I never actually walked in to that place! Yes, I was punished for a few weeks after that. The fact is that I wasn't doing anything wrong (well, other than lying to my parents!) I mean, I wasn't drinking alcohol or doing drugs.

I have not been back to Iran for more than three decades, but I hear that young people's lives are very hard and very complicated after the Islamic revolution came to power. Apparently, very quickly, they started enforcing the thousand year old Islamic laws onto young people's lives, which meant no contact between boys and girls unless they were siblings or married. As a result, a lot of young girls became targets for the local Islamic police, were arrested and even raped behind the closed doors of jails, under the name of Islam and God.

A lot of young men received beatings and were even raped under the same circumstances, after being arrested at a party or gathering with mixed gender youngsters and where alcoholic beverages were found.

We lived and breathed music back in the seventies. There was western music for those who understood it and all kinds of other music for everybody. Even the most fanatic families would enjoy some sort of Persian folk music. The first thing that the Islamic government took away from people was music. As they described in many of their baseless television and radio talk shows, music is the way of the devil to sneak into people's souls. So, listening to music, God forbid moving your body to it, drinking alcohol, talking and laughing with members of the other sex, touching the hand of someone of the other sex, women showing their hair or the skin above the wrist or ankle, eating pork…all became a crime (not a taboo, but a major crime) that was fought with severe punishment by the government.

I hear from Iranian friends and a relative that now, boys and girls do mingle and girls let their hair show a little on top of their foreheads. I also hear that due to extreme financial problems in Iran, sex has become a very common method for gaining some extra cash and a high percentage of the population is addicted to opium, as it is more easily and cheaply obtained than alcoholic beverages. I hear that university teachers openly ask for sex from female students in exchange for passing grades. So, it is evident that people who thought an Islamic government would push that society towards living more modestly were highly mistaken.

I read in the world news that the Islamic government of Iran has been severely stopping Baha'i students from having any college education and has even been arresting those teachers who decide to teach and guide these youngsters outside the universities and colleges. I do agree that the way the Shah was ruling Iran was not the answer to solving the economic and cultural problems of the country, but we had no idea that by pushing his establishment out we would get these 'animals' forcing our country back in time, into the Middle Ages. There are many discussions and ideas about this very subject.

Some believe that the Shah's controlling power wasn't good enough for his western big brothers and it was time to pull him out. Some believe that growing leftist ideologies among young people became a red light for the western countries to decide to bring an Islamic government into power to stop Iran's population from mental growth, and make it impossible for any socialist ideology to flourish in Iran. Others believe that in the gambling game between two big western powers Iran was given to one for the price of its other neighbors… I will leave you dear reader to do your own research, if you wish, and come up with your own answer to this political mayhem in Iran.

When I look back I see that what Shah was trying to do wouldn't work anyway, because of the majority's mentality about religion and gender difference. The environment I grew up in wasn't the real society of Iran; it was just for those who wanted to believe that we were a free society. Deep in the same city there were girls who were getting beaten to death by their father or brothers for talking to a man and there were women who were quietly accepting their husband's second or even third marriage in the same household. I knew of a man who was married to two sisters for more than twenty years and they were all living together as one happy family! How sick is that?

Back to my personal memories…

Memories of Mom

Mom was a beautiful woman and she knew it! She had big hopes and wishes. When she was a child, she wanted to go to London, to be an actress. "Over my dead body," her mother had said; "You aren't going anywhere." She wanted to be a nurse, but her family wouldn't allow that either. Mom was the only female in her family to continue with further education after high school, and she became an elementary school teacher.

Mom was such a positive person about everything, to the extent that it was sometimes difficult to verify if she really didn't get it, or she was so nice that she didn't want to see the dark side of a person or situation.

Always smiling and singing, she took classes in opera, the accordion and Persian folk singing. After having us children, she went back to school, when I was about 10 years old, to get her Bachelor's Degree. Apparently, that's when the trouble started in our house. Some family and friends have told me that it's been said that when she started paying attention to school, and singing classes, and not to her husband, that's when her husband went astray and found another woman.

I honestly don't know how accurate that is, whether it really was the reason or not. But I don't think that it was the reason, because a true husband and wife are best friends and they protect each other and back each other up.

My mother around 1960, Tehran

I would sit on my mother's bed, watching her putting her makeup on; just looking at her and admiring her. She'd put false eyelashes on and then spray her face after making it up, with some sort of fixative to keep the makeup in place.

Mom was so beautiful, even after her fifties. She confided in me that that was one of the reasons why she couldn't believe my father cheated on her.

"I'd look in the mirror and wonder 'how can it be possible?'" she said. She was either naïve or just had too nice a heart so she couldn't believe the things that happened in her life.

I wasn't close to Mom; I was closer to Dad. Mom felt that her mother hadn't loved her enough. In a domino effect, she transmitted that feeling to me. I felt that my mother didn't like me much, as she was very light-skinned with dirty blond hair (due to her Russian Jewish blood) and I was very dark skinned; even among Iranians, I'm the darkest. I always felt that she wasn't happy or satisfied, in fact, that she was disappointed that I wasn't as pretty or European looking as her. By the time I got to 13 years of age, self-protection had unfortunately kicked in, and I refused to allow myself to get close to Mom.

While still married to my dad, who was also married to someone else, and after all the ups and downs in her marriage, Mom left Iran. I don't know what she was thinking; maybe she thought things would get better from a distance – if you don't touch, it will get better. What was she thinking, leaving without solving the situation?

Mom left Iran for Italy where my sister was at the time. After 'grabbing' my sister, she went to the USA where my brother and uncle were already living, in Pennsylvania. Mom continued to be married to a man, who loved and was married to another woman, for the next thirty years. I remained angry at her for not fighting back, for not claiming her place – either kick him out of her life forever or work on bringing him back.

Mom was actually in her seventies when she divorced Dad. She didn't want to die married to a man who was also married to another woman. I actually loved Mom very much, but I didn't believe in her... I don't know how much of an effect this had on my mental and emotional growth. I have come to the conclusion that the relationship I had with her was a contribution towards the complex that I developed over the years, of always being the second choice, second best... My dad preferred to be with another woman and family; my husband would rather be with his organization than with me; even my second husband has a family from a first marriage.

Back to Mom; she was a very avant-garde person – ahead of her time. Back then, raising children was at the stage where children should not speak until they were spoken to. Mom believed that children had rights and would tell us to talk about our feelings or share our feelings in writing. She would sing for us. She would show us the sky at sunset and ask how many colors we could see. Mom loved art and had an eye for art. She wanted her children to do something in the field of art. Both my brother and I are both good at drawing and portraits, and I feel that is thanks to Mom.

Mom handing the graduates their diplomas -- Mid 1950's.

Mom was determined to raise her children differently to how she was raised. She gave us lots of space to speak out, and for my sister and me, to be the women that we are. This was partly due to her not having a father to 'protect' her. She was 'protecting' herself and encouraged us to do the same. As a result, my sister and I are rather different to many Iranian women of that era —we are outspoken go-getters... We have been questioned by US friends: How come you two are so outspoken? Aren't women in Iran always under the control of men? The Islamic rulers would like to think that!

Of course, there were Muslims who were different to us, but Iran has been a mixture of many cultures. We were free – talking to boys, holding hands, going to parties. Some girls weren't allowed to talk to boys. I had a friend who was beaten up by her mother and brother because she had spoken to a boy in the street.

There may have been a mixture of cultures living together, but I refuse to believe that the Iran of the last, say two hundred years was a corner of the Earth with women constantly walking about in fear and men doing whatever they wanted to them. I absolutely refuse that. Mom was a free woman who dressed and socialized as she wanted. Even my dad's mother, who grew up in a strict Muslim family, and covered her hair, rode horses and hunted. She would stand on the horse to shoot!

So, even from a religious perspective, women weren't a suppressed gender. This new Islamic regime is something that has been recently forced on Iran's people. The suppression is not deep rooted in Iran. If you look back through history, queens ruled the country. The Zoroastrian government was ruled by men and women. Iran had women who went to war. For me, women and men working together is the true colorful Iran;

the oppressive government needs to be plucked out of Iran to allow her to live again as a fully functioning organ in the Earth body.

Memories of Auntie Nour

Mom was the third child in the family of four girls and one boy. Someone who I hold very dearly in my heart is Mom's older sister, Auntie Nour. She was a great influence in my life in Iran. Nour would sing to us children and was a very spiritual, upbeat woman who could often be heard laughing out loud. Although she was very religious she didn't lecture people. Always happy to help anyone, Nour was loved by all around her.

Unfortunately, she had a miscarriage and then had to have a hysterectomy due to a tumor. So she didn't become a mother to her own children, but was a natural mother to all children. Her beloved cocker spaniel became her surrogate child which received Nour's love just as her own child would have. She was born a mother… As a Sunday school teacher, Nour's teaching of the Baha'i concepts involved lots of fun. She loved to walk along holding her nieces' hands and we loved walking with her too.

Nour and her husband moved to London three times, but always returned as they couldn't cope with the homesickness. In Iran, Nour was an active member of the community, being part of a group who would visit the villages bringing aid to whoever needed it.

At home, she was a wonderful homemaker. She made sweaters and dresses; Nour would make dresses for me and tell me that I could be a pretty young lady… Her hands always had to be at work. After making pickles, she would take them to people as gifts, or people would bring her fruit so that she could make jelly. I consider this upbeat, happy, straight forward and good-natured lady an angel. She was a peacemaker, even in her own family – between my mom and their older sister. I loved Nour so much.

When Nour and her husband were arrested, the captors rushed the house, breaking down the doors and shooting their beloved dog. Nour knew the arrest would happen. She had given her jewelry to a woman neighbor to pass on to her sisters once she was dead.

During her detention, Nour was tortured. One of my aunts, Pari would visit her twice a week. I couldn't visit her because my husband was an active revolutionist. Every visit, Auntie Nour would sit on her hands and always wore a scarf. She sat on her hands to ease the pain in her bottom due to the daily lashes she received. When she removed the scarf, she was black and blue around her throat. She would be coughing blood. Part of the torture consisted of immersion in cold, then hot, then cold, then hot water… as well as the lashes.

Dear Nour was a housewife, pro-humanity, not the satanic spy for the Israelis she was accused of being in the papers. She was Baha'i; that was her only 'crime' and she refused to say that she was Muslim. So what happened to Ayatollah's promises before he hijacked the Iranian revolution and came to power? What happened to:

"In the Islamic Republic the rights of the religious minorities are respectfully regarded," as Ayatollah Khomeini stated in an interview with an Austrian television reporter in Paris, November, 1978?

What happened to:

"In the Islamic government all people have complete freedom to have any kind of opinion," as he put forward in an interview with Human Rights Watch, in the same period? Or:

"Our future society will be a free society, and all the elements of oppression, cruelty, and force will be destroyed." That was stated in an interview, during the same period in Paris, with the German magazine "Der Spiegel".

I will tell you what happened. All those promises along with many others were distorted and then vanished when the Islamic regime came into power. Instead the promises became threats for the Iranian people.

In a speech in September, 1979, to the Iranian Air Force officers in Isfahan his threat was: "Do not interrupt the activities. You all have to obey the Islamic Republic. And if you don't, you all will vanish." And in a talk to the Representatives from Tabriz, Qom, in September, 1979 Ayatollah left no uncertainty in their minds over how he was going to act: "Those who are against us are like cancer tumors that need to be removed surgically; otherwise they will corrupt everything." Indeed non-Muslims were treated as criminals who were arrested, like Nour. In 1980 Ayatollah's message to the Iranian people was that there was no need to accuse these 'criminals' or give them a trial. They would receive no compassion as guilty parties and they would be killed...

Nour never complained about anything. On the last prison visit, she told her sister Pari that we all came to this world and we'll all leave sometime. It doesn't matter if we leave by choice or if we are taken early. "Keep your head high and tell all my nieces and nephews that I love them and have always loved them as my own."

Memories of Auntie Pari

While I'm talking about Mom and Auntie Nour, I'd like to mention their youngest sister, Auntie Pari. She's the youngest of five children who grew up without a father. Since she was the youngest she had more freedom, compared to her older sisters, to experience life outside of the shelter that was provided through her family. She grew up to be very street smart and I think her IQ was a bit higher than the rest of them too.

When Nour was in jail Pari, who had just lost her tall and handsome army husband in a horrific car crash, would visit her as much as she possibly could. They would lie about Nour's whereabouts just like they did for my husband, just to give folks a hard time. Pari would go to a particular jail in one city and, as they would send her to another address a hundred miles away, she would follow. I don't even think she had a car. I think she was using public transport.

Pari and her youngest son were actually in the car when her husband crashed it and was killed. She was in the hospital when we had to tell her that he would never come back. She was unable to even attend his funeral due to being in a hospital bed at the time.

There is no doubt in my mind that Pari is a very brave person for following her sister through the Islamic jails and showing them that they couldn't just make Nour disappear. The fact that she went there for the last time and Nour's husband told Pari to bring some tissues the next time, and she knew what he meant, is beyond me. He meant for wiping away the tears, of course, since they knew the day that they were about to be executed.

She recounted to me about when she wanted to claim the bodies. Both sides – the Muslim authorities and the Baha'i organization -- wanted her to drop it and walk away. The authorities were insulting her and her dead sister, telling her that there was no need to ask for the corpse. The Baha'i organization wanted her to calm down, fearing that her actions could have caused some angry decision by the authorities to kill whoever they had in custody.

I didn't know her well enough back then to know for sure, but there is a possibility that this all had an influence on how she behaves and feels today as the results of what she went through. In my case, I admit that I am scared of people and what they are capable of doing to me. I would imagine that Pari feels the same…

I do admire Parie's bravery. She is a tiger who steps forward as if she has nothing to lose. That's a family trait that I have too. I will share an example of Parie's bravery with you as an illustration. Her husband had died in the car crash. Pari had to leave Iran on her own, with her youngest child, an 8 year old boy. What was brave about that? She left Iran via the illegal route. That takes a lot of courage. She had to pass through a lot of borders into Pakistan, and Afghanistan, living there for several months. During this time, Pari had physical problems – bleeding – and she had to undergo surgery. So, before reaching the US she went through a lot.

She now leads a comfortable life and has done so since she reached the US and my uncle, her brother, took care of her. Auntie Pari now writes lots of memoirs; she has written hundreds of pages in Farsi, so that she doesn't forget. The danger of doing that as an older lady is that if she's mistaken about some events in the past, by writing them down, she creates a false memory. I know that Mom did that. I haven't read her memoirs and I'm not sure if everything that she writes down really happened. Or perhaps that was her perspective of what happened. It does give her an avenue of release.

One of the reasons why I wanted to approach my memoir now is so that I do it before I get too old and forget what exactly happened; I don't want to start talking about things my mind would have wanted to have happened. That is the danger I wish to step away from.

Memories of Dad

I adored my dad.

He came from a very poor family. His father had died when he was a baby and his older brother tried to be the man of the house and take care of the family. That caused a lot of resentment between Dad and my uncle; Dad didn't consider it my uncle's place to tell him what to do, but Uncle thought he was in charge.

Their father had been a poet – very poor but highly educated. He loved literature and both boys went to college and had advanced education. Dad obtained a Masters in Geography and History of the World.

His family was so poor that every morning, his mother would put a few pennies in his hand and tell him to go buy sugar cubes and tea leaves, along with half a loaf for that day. They couldn't shop in advance. Both brothers worked hard and became well-off and were able to take care of their mother, sisters, nieces and nephews.

I don't know how to explain Dad's attitude about the other woman, so I won't try. However, I would like to talk about this woman as a person, yet not in connection with her relationship with my father. I never met her (I only saw a picture of her standing next to my dad), but as she was a well-known name in Tehran's education system it was very easy to hear about her personality, physical appearance and way of life. She was a below average faced, tall, big boned woman (whereas my mother was a petite five foot two person). This woman was well-known for two distinct reasons; one was that she had told everybody that she used to be one of the Prince Reza Pahlavi's teachers (he couldn't have been more than 10 years old at that time). The other rumor was that she apparently had a shameless and vulgar way of talking. She was known as a well-read educated, yet dirty mouthed woman among her colleagues in the Iranian educational system at the time. She also never denied her ties to SAVAK, the Shah's secret service well-known and documented for torturing college students.

Dad was a very emotional, sensitive man who could understand other people's feelings. His heart was immense and he loved animals. He had sympathy for those less well-off than him and always believed in helping others. If he could share his money, he would.

However, he had a very harsh exterior; I think that was the only way he could protect himself. He had very macho behavior, and was often rather short in his interaction with others, with not much of a smile on his face. Little laughter came from Dad, but deep inside he was like a baby. I think I connected with that inner child.

He loved poetry and reading about what was going on in the world, the big powers and the logistics of other countries. On the other hand, he wasn't fond of books, novels or stories.

I always felt protected when I was around my dad. That's normal, I guess; Fathers are supposed to be protective. First daughters probably have that special connection with their fathers. As for me, as a 10 year old, Dad was always surprised by me. "You come out with things that are very old for your young years," he would say. That made me feel proud of myself. I felt special.

The reason why I didn't go astray as a teenager was Dad. He gave me a sense of morality where drugs and sex were concerned. It wasn't religion that guided me. Dad was my guide; he made me feel a better being for not going down those roads.

I also learned from him that it's good to have compassion. It's valuable to be able to see through the eyes of others. I actually practiced this on Dad himself when I was a grown woman – I tried to communicate with him about his betrayal of his marriage to Mom.

"Dad, when you came to the point where you didn't love my mom anymore, when you felt physically unable to have an intimate relationship with this woman anymore, why didn't you divorce her? She was young, in her forties. You found intimacy, love and friendship with the other woman. You denied that for my mom," I said to him.

"She could have started a new relationship, if you had released her, let her go. She could have started a new life – marriage, a boyfriend, love. But you didn't. You took that away from her…" I continued. His answer wasn't very mature! The answer that came from the father that I adored didn't satisfy me at all.

"What do you know daughter? Maybe, in my mind, I did the best." What he meant was that my mother wasn't strong enough to hold herself up, raise children, fight back and stand on her own feet, without my father's shadow in her life.

He lived a double life, keeping his existence in our lives, coming home every night, paying the bills, checking our school-work, vacations…

He provided for us, but he took his love and intimacy elsewhere. In his mind, he did the right thing by not abandoning us. I don't believe that. Mom was weak and not strong enough on her own to cope with a divorce, but she had family – my uncle and aunts in the USA. She would have taken us to the USA and maybe that's what Dad was afraid of. Dad couldn't bear to be away from us three children. So, maybe he knowingly or unknowingly sacrificed our mom just to be close to us children and be connected with us.

Dad was a hard-working man, a believer who worked for the Shah. His loyalty was never blind-sighted; he never behaved as if his superior was a god and he should follow the rules because the superiors said so. He questioned everything and everybody. Dad was the Minister for Education for the state of Tehran, and later for all the other states in Iran.

I can remember that even though we had a chauffeur, Dad would jump into a jeep and travel to the villages, early in the morning, checking the schools to see if the teachers arrived on time. He'd go unannounced to see what was going on in the schools, to see if the children were receiving the education they should. That wasn't part of his job: he could have sat at his desk in his office job, but that's the sort of person he was.

He could have ordered people to do this for him, or like many before and after him, in that position, he could have become rather rich by embezzling the construction budget. There would be a budget for building schools in certain towns, cities or villages. With some other ministers in his position, not all that budget would actually go to that school building project. Many of his fellow ministers were extremely rich. We were well-off because he lived off his salary alone and not funds from embezzlement. Dad stood proud in truthful living and would never do something where he wouldn't be able to look at himself in the mirror.

That sense of pride was certainly transferred to me.

When Mom came to the US she basically walked away from an unbearable situation – Dad's double life and the lack of intimacy between Mom and Dad. My brother was already in Pennsylvania and Mom and my sister joined him. After their departure, I lived with Dad. My mother wasn't there during my married life or when I became a mother. Dad was there. When I was pregnant and doing hospital visits, it was Dad who sat with me; he would hand me the bottle for the baby.

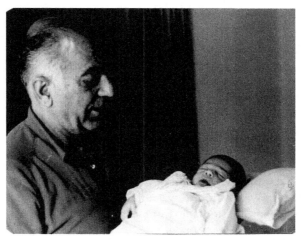

My dad holding my newborn son. Tehran 1981

Thus, I developed an extra loving connection with Dad after the rest of the family had moved to the US. So, it appeared to the family in the US that I was condoning Dad's double life, backing him. The feeling was that the other family members had taken another opposing side.

My sister and brother didn't connect with Dad, especially my sister because she was very young when Dad went 'astray' and wasn't emotionally connected to us as a family anymore. My brother felt betrayed because he felt that he should protect his mom. Thus a line of separation developed between us. Up to this day, I feel different. It's as if my sister and brother are on one side, the side where our mom stood while she was alive, and I'm on another side, with a view on life, personality and standards somewhat similar to my dad.

So, that was Dad…his values, mistakes, emotional decisions in life and his courage to do what his heart told him to do, meanwhile stepping on other people's lives and hearts, especially my mom's.

###

My First Car

I had just turned 19 and really wanted a car. I knew Dad had deposited some money in our bank accounts every year ever since we were born, so I knew the amount in my savings account.

That day I grabbed my savings account booklet and took a cab to the bank. I asked the bank teller for 200,000 Rilas (about 3000 US dollars at that time). I had my birth certificate with me too to prove my age! The teller asked me to wait for a few minutes and after about twenty minutes I

was guided to the bank manager's office. He was a nice man in his fifties in a gray suit, behind a large desk. He asked me to have a seat and said:
"Miss Azita, why do you need all of this money?"
"I want to buy a car," I answered, looking him straight in the eyes.
"Does your father know you are here?"
"No, I'm at the legal age to withdraw money from my account," I said holding out my birth certificate towards him.
"How about you come back tomorrow and we will give you the money then?" he suggested with a diplomatic smile.

I understood; he had called my dad and my dad had told him not to give me the money! An argument with the bank manager wouldn't be a smart move as my dad was influential enough to control all the rules and regulations to stop me from having the money. I left the bank feeling helpless and disappointed.

That night everybody was very quiet at the dinner table. Finally, Dad turned to me and said:
"So, you were at the bank today?"
"Yes, I was, but they didn't let me withdraw from my own bank account."
"I put that money in your bank account. You didn't. You can withdraw money when you are the one who puts it in there," he said calmly. "Why do you need that much money anyway?"
"I *need* a car," I said, trying to look as sad as possible. "All my classmates come to school with their *own* cars. I'm tired of getting a ride from Mimi. Sometimes she wants to go out with her boyfriend and I feel so embarrassed that she has to drive me home first, when her boyfriend is sitting in the car with us." I knew *that* would do the trick. My dad wouldn't want me to be in the car with a young couple who had no business to hang out together anyway!
"How about I buy you the car you want and we won't touch your bank account?" he suggested as he poured ice water into his glass.

I was very happy and sincerely thanked Dad. I requested a small French car. Life became much easier for me and Polad after I got my car. I didn't have to catch a ride to and from college and I didn't have to stand at the corner of the street waiting for a cab.

Chapter Four

How Did it Happen?

It was a good thirty minute drive from my parent's house to school and every day I would happily drive my little car to school, feeling content with my life except for one thing -- being in love with someone who didn't trust me at all. (We'll look at that later). Polad had a side of his life that I wasn't very close to. I knew that his mind was different from those whom I had around me. His way of thinking was spreading more and more in our country and soon I started hearing his version of the story from some kids in college too.

College Years

My school was a small private college of languages. My major was English as a Second Language. There were mostly well off kids in that school who just needed to obtain some college degree. Also, there were a minority of students who were really trying to get a degree so they could work and pay the bills. These students were from other states than the capital and not from financially established families.

I used to have classes both in the morning and afternoon and I got a part-time job, via my dad's help, in the "Construction Establishment Center" which was a government office. It was just clerical work but the pay was very good! Every Wednesday I would just skip work and go to the beauty salon and on Thursdays the vice president's secretary would tell me to sign the employee's daily book for both days, as if I was present there the day before! At the time, I never thought to be special and didn't pay any attention to all of those exceptions and privileges in my life. I guess us three children, especially my sister and I, were so sheltered in our lives that we didn't realize how well we were taken care of.

###

One summer, Dad agreed to send my mom, my sister and I to Europe to travel and shop. I was 19 and very happy about that trip. I had been with Polad for two years by then and I could see he was not very happy about me not being around for the whole summer. Later on, Dad told me that he purposely did that so I could see the world before settling down for life with the first boy that I met.

In the hotel lobby in Rome, Italy with my mom and sister (1976)

That trip was just wonderful. We traveled to Rome, Italy and stayed in a very nice hotel in Veneto Street. It was just a walking distance from our hotel to the downtown and all of those mind-blowing stores. We enjoyed the side walk cafés at night and going to the museums, historical sites and shops during the day. I bought a large suitcase full of leather shoes, boots and handbags! We also took a day tour to Napoli and another one to Capri. I was so taken by the sun still being in the sky at 9 p.m. in Capri, and all of the caves that the boatman took us to.

One afternoon I came down to the hotel bar by myself to have a soda and smoke a cigarette. Another customer who was having a drink asked me where I was from. When I told him that I was from Iran, he asked if my family was as rich as the Shah (Iran's king). I was confused by his question. I didn't hear the sarcasm in his voice or see the smirk on his face. "Of course not," I replied with a polite smile. "My dad is well off but we aren't *that* rich." I never thought we were, until years later when I saw how the rest of the people were living in Tehran.

The guy said that all Iranians must be very rich from selling the oil to the world and at that point I suddenly saw the sarcasm and told him: "Well, you know, we build schools, roads and hospitals with the money we get from selling the oil." I knew that wasn't entirely true, but I figured I had to defend my country and the government of which my father was a big part.

After two weeks we flew to the UK and visited my cousin who was going to school in London. He was sent to England by himself when he was 16, so it was great to see him again. Mom took him with us for a little shopping and we all had a great time in a large indoor shopping center, which was as large as a town.

Then we flew to Germany to stay with Mom's cousins who had been Dusseldorf residents for years. The two brothers and their dad, who was Mom's uncle, had a rug business there. Mom had a lot of relatives in Germany and everybody was very nice to us. We were invited to many parties and even a few top scale dance clubs. My sister, who was almost 16 at the time, and I had a great time in Germany, but we were a little confused by the openness of boys' and girls' relationships in the streets. One evening, when we were walking around in an amusement park some young guys and girls approached us and wanted us to mingle with them, but we passed and rapidly walked away, thinking wow, they looked just like the teens on television and in movies.

Years later, I realized that we were in the heart of Europe during the mid-seventies and had really missed out on what was happening in the world! I don't mean sex, drugs and rock and roll, but at least we could have seen what was happening and become a little educated... instead of being so sheltered.

After being with friends and family in Germany for a few weeks we took a day tour to Denmark and enjoyed a boat ride on the river.

When we came back home I was in no rush to see Polad! The honest truth was that I hadn't missed him that much. I was embarrassed to think that way and felt really bad that while I was traveling and having fun, he was stuck with working hard to pay his bills and going to school at the same time.

I guess I had grown up or maybe my self-esteem had flourished because I could see that guys were noticing me and girls wanted to hang out with me. Polad was getting angrier with me over simple things such as my make-up, my perfume or what I was wearing. Sometimes even over what I said or who I talked to. Our fights were getting worse and even occasionally physical. I was always accused of acting too loose and not showing that I was 'taken'. One day, when I was in college, Polad entered; he walked towards me and said: "Let's go." I told him that I still had classes and couldn't leave, so he left without hesitating to openly show his anger and disappointment.

Later on my father told me that he heard that my boyfriend came to my school and ordered me to leave with him and I followed him like a slave! "Wow; so my dad has people spying on me in school too!" I thought. I knew Polad had people watching me in school, but I didn't realize Dad was doing the same thing.

###

It was the fall of 1976 when I returned from our summer trip to Europe. That year, when I went to my classes, I realized that the atmosphere had changed. I really felt the difference between 'them' and 'us'. It is horrible to put it that way, but it was true. There were those students who were there to get a degree, to be able to hold a job to feed their families; and there was 'us' who just wanted to have fun, dress up and learn another language, so we could read more books and would be more comfortable while shopping in Europe.

With Polad being so deeply in my life by then, I could not hang around with my old friends and I had to make some major changes in my appearance. The news about protests in Tehran and other major cities of Iran were coming more openly. Although the newspapers never printed the truth, people knew what was going on through others via word of mouth.

We had no email or electronic media connections, but the words were travelling from this house to the next within one night. We would find out that the night before soldiers had shot hundreds of school kids who were demonstrating against the Shah in such and such a street. The newspapers, television and radio stations would immediately deny the news. All we had to do was go to that street and see the small bloody hand prints on the walls and the bullet holes next to them.

The government announced Martial Law in Tehran and all other large cities. People could not form groups of more than three at a time in the streets. Soldiers had the right to shoot people after 4 p.m. if they were seen in the streets. Yet, the demonstrators would walk the streets in the heart of the dark nights and we could clearly hear the bullet sounds and people's screams, from our front porch.

I knew Polad was in every one of those demonstrations and I was in constant fear for his life. Polad and I were living on two different sides of Tehran, so I wouldn't always know where he was or if he was okay. He used to call me from public phones just to say hello, and I used to impatiently wait for those phone calls every day.

At first, the news of what had happened during the street demonstrations the day or night before was all transmitted by a few political groups in Iran. There were Islamic groups who believed in a fair economy for all. There were Socialist groups who believed in arming the civilians to fight back against the government, and then there were Socialist groups who were opposed to that.

These groups would arrange demonstrations and people would show up and join them in the streets. After a while, regular people who had something in common would gather to walk in the streets together at an arranged time. It could be a gathering of high school kids from one area, for instance, or the students from one university, or workers from a particular factory... I can easily claim with my hand on my heart that 99.9% of those demonstrations were peaceful. Nobody was armed except the Shah's soldiers.

There were different stages over the two years. When the first demonstrators were out or were shot, probably eighty percent of the population was completely unaware. I wouldn't have known if it hadn't been for my connection with Polad.

As demonstrations became more common, we would be in the streets in groups, starting with about one hundred people. We'd march along in groups chanting: "Death to Shah. Freedom, freedom, or kill me." As we marched from street to street, chanting these slogans in one voice, more people would join until there would be two hundred, three hundred or four hundred demonstrators.

At one of the corners or intersections someone would begin running, screaming "Soldiers!" Now, the first reaction wouldn't be to run away. In fact, we were organized. The girls would group together in the middle, with the boys, arm in arm, forming a human chain around us, advancing like a big ball, towards another intersection.

Gas bombs would be launched into the mass of people, and we'd lose grip of each other. Running in different directions, not knowing where the people we came with had gone, we'd desperately try to grab each other, to be able to stay together. The greatest fear was to be separated from everyone else – you didn't want to be alone. That's when they would capture you, and take you in for torture, to discover the leaders of your organization who had instigated the demonstration.

I was among the demonstrators, on occasions, when the soldiers lined up and shot at us. The first group of people fell down and the rest of us ran about in different directions. It wasn't out of fear – it was a 'rush' – a feeling of being invincible; you could shake and tease this big giant, this dictator, the army and all the automatic weapons they had. It was a rush and, believe it or not, there was an element of fun.

Having said that, my sister and I witnessed a young man, of about twenty-one, receive a bullet in his front. The soldiers were using the famous G3 automatic machine guns. Apparently, the bullet turns around on itself extremely fast as it flies forward, so when it hits its target, it's still turning. The result in this case was a two inch point of entry hole in the man's front and a football sized gaping exit point in his back!

An ambulance arrived. As people were trying to pull him onto a stretcher, he gathered all the power he had to pull his upper body up, raise his fist above his head, and scream: "Death to the dictator!" As he shouted, blood gushed from his back, so that it was streaming from the stretcher.

That experience was something else. I grew up in that moment. I realized that there are bigger things to worry about in the world, and how easily a human being's life could go down the drain! You are here now, but you may not be here tomorrow…

I would go to school and there would be empty chairs around me. They had been following this or that group, and we guessed that they had been shot or "got". We hoped that they had been shot dead, rather than been taken. You didn't want them to get you and torture you.

The soldiers became more and more visible as the revolution progressed beyond half way. They even brought tanks into the streets of Tehran…

Reza Shah was the first Pahlavi king of Iran who somewhat helped the country to grow. He also ordered the construction of a special prison just for his political opponents, in the heart of Tehran. This building was designed and built by a German architect in 1932. During Mohamad Reza Shah's ruling this prison was called the "Anti-Sabotage Joint Committee", or *Komiteh Moshtarak*. The Shah also built another detention center that is called Evin Prison, which is an equally horrific place to be at. During all of the sixty or seventy years of use nobody in the neighboring buildings knew what was going on in the "Komiteh Moshtarak". Nobody could hear the hundreds of men and women being tortured or killed in that building due to its special cylindrical design. The Islamic government changed its name to "Towhid Prison" and used it until 2000, when it was shut down due to many reports to the International Human Rights Organizations. After that it was turned into a museum and called "Ebrat Museum", depicting the brutality that took place here during the Shah's regime, as if the present regime is not doing the same crimes to the innocent children of Iran, in Evin or many other political prisons that they have built…

"LONELY PLANET REVIEW, Iran Ebrat Museum

There is nothing subtle about the Iran Ebrat Museum, a one-time prison of the shah's brutal secret police that now exhibits that brutality with an equal measure of pro-revolution propaganda. The prison is an incongruously attractive building, with wings radiating from a circular courtyard. But what went on here was not attractive at all.

During the 1970s, hundreds of political prisoners – including several prominent clerics and post-revolutionary figures whose names you will recognize from street signs – were held in tiny cells and, in many cases, tortured by the Anti-Sabotage Joint Committee, a branch of the despised Savak (National Intelligence and Security Organization). The various functions of the prison are dramatically re-created with waxwork dummies and liberal doses of red paint. The shah's henchmen are depicted wearing neckties (a pro-Western symbol in modern Iran) and looking brutish (check the eyebrows). The propaganda element is emphasized with numerous photos of the former royal family – just in case you forget who was responsible.

Propaganda aside, this prison was undoubtedly a terrible place to end up and the people running it guilty of brutality on a grand scale. It's just a pity that the abhorrence of torture and politically motivated incarceration expressed here is not shared by the current ruling regime; stories from Tehran's notorious Evin Prison are just as horrifying."

Source of above article: http://www.lonelyplanet.com/iran/tehran/sights/museums-galleries/iran-ebrat-museum

When tanks rolled through the streets of Iran and the soldiers started shooting at people, some of those political groups made it possible for civilians to raid the Iranian army locations and walk out with machine guns. There were hand guns and machine guns all over Tehran --American G3 and Russian Kalashnikov became household names. In some houses, people would sit around in the evening having tea, chatting and loading bullets in their machinegun magazines to have them ready for the next day's street battles.

News would arrive about this and that town which had reached the point of "freedom" from the local police and about other ones that were falling as the Shah's army would arrive at their borders. The night that tanks were supposed to enter Tehran through the "Azadie Square", we were there laying in the gutters, waiting for them with Molotov Cocktails. What a night that was!

All the political groups were following information and orders from their own sources. Polad had come home and said that the news was that they were trying to bring tanks to Tehran to stop the demonstrators. The army had requested small, but effective tanks. I followed his lead.

We were all dressed in a way so as not to shine in the night – we covered our hair, put soot on our faces, under our eyes so that part of our face wouldn't shine if car headlamps caught our faces. Our clothes were dark and we wore gloves. We spent all night lying in the open-top gutters, prepared for an attack.

"We" were members from all the different groups. You could guess a person's ideology from how they dressed and spoke. There were some

Mujahideen members, Leftist Muslim university students who believed in equality when it comes to finances and economy. The Shah called them Islamic Marxists. (I don't know what became of the Mujahideen later on. I hear about killings, kidnappings and attacks, but I have no idea if the Mujahideen that we knew then were the original source of the Mujahideen in the Middle East and around the world now, but they could be. Back then, their full name was the People's Mujahideen Organization of Iran). The girls in that group covered their hair and believed in Islam; they prayed, but carried weapons against the Shah, because they believed a true Muslim, by following the Quran could actually be more sympathetic towards the poor than the Shah's government was.

The way they dressed made them stand out as members of the Mujahideen group. Polad's group leaned more towards a free socialist Iran. There were also groups leaning towards Russian government. We were all lying down in the gutters together waiting for these tanks. There was a feeling of the 'rush' and fear (would the tanks drive right over us?). We waited throughout the night, but it didn't happen! At about 5 a.m. we disbanded and went our own ways. The tanks did actually come through the street, but in the middle of the day.

For those of us who weren't much involved with the political activities and the history of those who were captured, tortured and killed in the past, a lot of those demonstrations were definitely full of a feeling of the rush. I believe that behind everyone who stands out from the crowd and screams NO, there's some kind of a psychological difference – a desire to be looked at, to be famous. I hope you see what I mean. I'm not saying that that is a sin, either, but I did see that element... Perhaps that is their reason for being here. Their purpose, mission could be filling them with the passion to stand out and say "look at me".

When I came to the US, I said to some of the Americans that back in the sixties and seventies, they had the social revolution with the drugs, sex and rock 'n roll and we overthrew the leaders of our country!

Little by little, we started hearing about an old Mullah from decades past who was against the Shah. It seemed that the other side of the population who weren't much involved with the younger and more educated part of the society liked him. We felt that it wouldn't hurt to back him up since his name was enticing a whole lot more people into the streets of Iran.

Well, I believe that that was our first mistake. The man's name was Khomeini and he was sending messages to the people of Iran from some village in France – Neauphle-le-Château! Wow, it was interesting to see that all of those small groups could fight the unfair government of Shah together under one umbrella. His name was bringing aid in the form of people and money, lots of money and that was a good thing, right? Wrong! But we couldn't see how wrong we were back then.

Soon the demonstrations became larger and larger. All over the country, people were carrying Khomeini's pictures during the demonstrations. The active political groups who had started the original movement against the Shah began to argue among themselves as to whether we should back this Mullah or not. The final decision was to back him up just as a way of getting through the situation in Iran, since people seemed to like him.

Khomeini jumped on that fast train, as it were and changed the Iranian revolution from the democratic route to an Islamic one. He couldn't have done that without some major financial and propaganda aid from those countries who were terrified to see that the civil war in Iran could have continued for many years and that Iran could very possibly become a Socialist country. They had to wrap the revolution up along with the very possible outcome that frightened them. What could have done that better than religion?

I feel a rant coming on. Bear with me for a short while as I release this from my being... My little rant may well give you some insight into the background of the situation, from my perspective. I've been asked if I wondered what it was all for, and was it worth it? When the revolution was happening it wasn't in the name of a religious government taking over Iran. It all began because the Shah was selling the oil, which belonged to future generations, in exchange for junk imported from other countries. It wasn't his money or even our money. It was Iran's children's and their children's money. The goal was to prevent the Shah from wasting our national treasure – oil. Reports came out stating that if he continued selling the oil at the same rate it would be completely depleted within fifty years.

He was a member of OPEC and would say how he had raised the price of the oil and he wouldn't let the Western countries take advantage of us. It wasn't about that. It was about: - if you want Iran to grow, the answer is not selling the oil and importing junk; the answer is to educate people, teach them how to farm, how to develop industrial manufacturing etc. so as to make and create what the country needed at the time, instead of selling the oil, to have revenue to be able to buy products from outside.

A great number of the products being brought in were items that the Western countries couldn't use themselves, such as outdated antibiotics and outdated baby formula. The Shah was giving the oil away. The Shah, his family and friends were accumulating money in offshore accounts. So, Iranians weren't receiving anything while everything was being sold, by a man who thought he was the shadow of God in Iran. His father had done some good acts for our country, but this man was bad news. He was pretending that Iran was advancing, by throwing grand international parties, while eight streets down, people didn't have the money to buy dinner or shoes...

The Shah was showing off on the surface, creating a façade. Maybe, deep inside he was trying to raise Iran and make it look different from the other backward-seeming Middle-Eastern countries – in the nature of, we are better because Iranians have national pride. That is important to Iranians. We are not Arabs. We are not Afghans. We are not Pakistanis. We are Iranians. Maybe inside he was trying to do good, but his approach was wrong. He was creating a bigger and deeper gap between those who had a lot and those with nothing. That gap between the classes could only lead to disaster.

Thus, at the time, the overall agreement was that we needed to kick out this man. We wanted a government where every four years everyone could vote for it. If the person voted in fell short of expectations, someone else could be voted in to govern for at least another four years. That was our dream.

Little by little, different groups grew up against the Shah. One was socialist, connected to the Soviet Union; one was socialist connected to China; one was following Lenin and another Stalin; one group believed that everyone should be given guns to fight with the soldiers, while another believed that civilians should be defended, but not be handed guns; others believed that religion shouldn't be totally taken out of the equation, (you could still be Muslims, Jews, or Christians), and so on... But the economy needed to change and the people should have had more say in how the oil was sold or not sold, and what should come into the country in exchange.

Universities should have been easier to enter. People should have had freedom to read about different ideas and ideologies. We were pushing for a Western type of society. The problem arose when the leftist political groups began telling the public that the Western society they were pushing for wasn't something that would improve Iran. The middle classes would still have power and the lower classes would remain poor. Thus, the Western-type government wasn't the answer. These groups decided that Iran needed a socialist government. All the socialist groups began getting closer to each other, except the Muslim kids, who believed you could follow your religion, but belong to all types of economies. This is the group the Shah called the Islamic Marxists. They called themselves Mujahedin...they stayed away from the socialist groups.

Outside Iran, the 'World' realized that the Iranian uprising was out of their control. The situation was getting out of hand. Up to that point Iran had been a bridge, an ally, and the Western countries didn't want that ally to escape from their hands. We believe that Western countries like the USA, Germany and others gathered together and brainstormed a solution. What could break this wave of socialism and be liked by the people, and even attract them? Their answer was religion, Islam to be exact. What am I saying? I'm saying that Khomeini was 'created' by the Western countries.

He was a poor mullah with nothing, who had been exiled by the Shah about twenty years earlier. Suddenly this old man showed up in Neauphle-le-Château, a village in France.

Where did he get the money from to go there? All the television and international journalists went there to interview him and listen to him. Who arranged that? Gradually, the rich Iranian merchants in the Grand Bazaar, in Tehran, grouped together to send funding to back this mullah. Why would they do that? Because if the socialists came to power, the first to be squashed would be the great money-makers of the Bazaar. The wealthy Iranians would lose grip on the people. When this wealthy group began backing Khomeini financially, the Western countries got what they wanted. With their funding too, Khomeini gained power. He was probably told that they didn't want Iran becoming socialist, and they were sure that he'd want Iran to become a good Muslim country, along the lines of: "Here's the money. Now go do it. We're all backing you…"

That was during the last few months of the revolution. We were all surging forward blindfolded. As we began to see, we couldn't believe it. Later on, during a lecture, Khomeini said that Iran's revolution was a train going very fast, and we jumped off right on time. That's just about the only true thing he ever stated! The revolution had begun two years before with no intention of following any religion. It was about the people rising up. Iran was heading towards the prospect of being socialist, and this would be dangerous for the Western countries, as well as the wealthy Bazaar businessmen. Khomeini was thus a puppet created by the Western countries…

Rant is over… Back to my personal story…

Everything was changing so fast in Iran and in my life. I had a car, my boyfriend and a circle of friends in school. I was living a very strange life. My family and my college friends didn't know anything about Polad's activities. That was how it was with those who were politically active. It was extremely dangerous to say something stupid to a family member, not knowing where it could have been repeated.

My sister had her own life with her boyfriend and her circle of friends and I had mine. We weren't sharing much back then, since we really didn't see each other that much. There were no sisterly talks or sharing of car-rides even though I had a car. I think she was probably taking cabs all over Tehran or maybe her boyfriend was giving her rides. I learned how to be quiet, instead of talking, and not to say anything that could have harmed Polad. Shah's secret service, SAVAK was extremely active and you could never know if your neighbor or best friend's sister or brother could cause you or your loved ones some serious trouble.

Chapter Five

Celebration Among the Turmoil
"Khastegary" (When the boy's family comes to the girl's house to ask for her hand in marriage)

June 1978

I was brimming over with excitement and trying to prepare our house to make it look as nice and clean as possible… While I'm talking about that time, I will describe my childhood house which was a beautiful large one. The yard had a tall metal door that my father would lock with three locks every night before going to bed. There were seven foot high walls around the yard which kept us safe and private. The yard wasn't that large, but large enough for us kids to run around and play in, and later on for parking two cars.

At the front of the house, a set of five wide steps lead up to the front porch, which extended right across the front of the house. Two columns made of large green mountain-rocks at the top of the steps seemed to be holding up the balcony above the porch! As children, I remember my brother and I used to play with our roller skates on the front porch and oh how we giggled as we skated back and forth.

Upon entering the house you came into a small entrance hallway that was intended for leaving our coats and muddy shoes. From there, you would walk into the large hallway with six doors (including the mud room's door) opening on to it. On the left was our TV room; after that was the large kitchen which was made up of two areas. One had cabinets and the dining table and the other was the cooking area with the stove, washer and the sink. The entire ceiling over the cooking area was made of thick glass which allowed in a great deal of light for cooking and all of the plants that we had there. At the corner of the cooking area was a door to the back yard.

Returning to the main hallway, after the kitchen door there was the entrance to the down-stairs bathroom and wash up area which also had a door to the backyard. After the wash up door was a beautiful half circle stairway in the hallway leading to the upstairs bedrooms. Next to the stairway, the entire wall was specially designed with non-see-through glass windows which could be opened one by one to allow the air to flow into the house. This fully glass wall used to bring a lot of light into the house.

Back in the main hallway there were two more doors immediately after the twisting round stairway and next to the formal living and dining room doors. These two doors were normally closed and occasionally locked to us children!

The second floor consisted of four bedrooms and two bathrooms. There were more stairs leading to the third floor storage room and the flat roof which had another storage room on it. The upstairs bedrooms were around a play area which overlooked the main hallway on the floor below. I remember when we were very young and our parents had formal guests, they would close the baby gates to the stairway, but we were allowed to sit on that play area and watch the guests going to and fro from the formal living room.

My father had purchased this house from an Armenian architect who had built the house for his family back in the fifties. They had sold the house to my dad around 1962 when they moved to the United States. I had overheard from my father that the original owner used to work for the US government in Iran, in the large building behind the house. That building was nicknamed "Asleh Chahar" (the Fourth Element). At the time I had no idea what it meant. Years later, I heard from some people that it was a part of CIA operations in Iran, but some believed that it was an organization to improve education in under developed countries such as ours.

My mom had cleaned up the formal living room and opened the tall curtains for the sun to shine through. Our Victorian style furniture was polished and looked elegant. I knew all of that wasn't necessary, but Mom had to make everything look perfect, so I was just going with the flow. Polad's family, including his mother, older brother, Babak and his beautiful wife Sima were coming to our house to formally ask my parents for my hand in marriage for Polad. Nobody knew, except Polad and I, that we had had a big fight just that morning and I wasn't even sure if they would show up!

The yard's doorbell rang and I opened it. Here they were, and Polad was carrying a beautiful basket of flowers. My mom came to the steps and asked them to please come in. It was kind of funny because none of our families were that traditional, but I guess we felt we had to do it to make my dad happy, so it was a bit awkward.

"Well, we all know why we are here," said Babak looking at Polad and I with a big smile. "Let's get straight to the point and make it possible for these two young kids to start their lives together." I think at that point my dad felt as if it was his duty to make a speech, so he cleared his throat and said:

"We are very pleased and thankful that my daughter and your brother have been respectful and courteous in their relationship, and have waited to be legally married…"

I wanted to curl up and become as small as possible and just disappear! What the hell was that all about? Who else in the room was even thinking about that particular subject? Was he hinting that we had BETTER have done that?

I couldn't bring myself to look up at anyone else, and to this date I have no idea what anyone around the room was doing, or what expressions they all had on their faces after my father's speech. I kept my head bowed, looking at my feet, hoping that I wasn't blushing too much! Polad's mom stood up, approached me, and put a gorgeous gold rose pendant on a chain around my neck and kissed my forehead. My mom offered pastries and my dad looked at me meaningfully to hurry up and get our guests some tea.

We decided on the date for our engagement party and planned the wedding for three months later in the beautiful month of September in Tehran.

About one hundred and fifty guests were invited for our engagement party, which was held in our house and my mother organized the catering from a famous French restaurant complete with the serving crew. There were four large French-doors to the living room and formal living room which opened onto the porch. By opening all those doors we could easily have the entire first floor open for one hundred and fifty guests. My mom had even asked our old butler, who had worked for us when I was an infant, to come over to help.

I looked very pretty in a tailor-made pink dress and Polad looked very handsome in his black suit. The hired photographer was doing an excellent job in capturing every moment of the party. My brother, who had been a Philadelphia resident for many years, came home for a short visit. After many years, I had the chance to see my cousins and Polad's siblings, who had come back from Europe and the US just to attend our engagement party.

My mother and I went to the old market in Tehran and she picked the fabric. Then we went to a tailor and ordered this dress based on my mom's design.

    Meanwhile, Iran was in turmoil with an unhappy population that was desperately seeking a way to be heard. There were different groups, different ideologies with one goal -- having a better government than the one the Shah had been enforcing on Iranians for years. Every evening, right after dusk, we could hear the demonstrators and then the sounds of bullets from Shah's army shooting the civilians. At the break of dawn the fire trucks would wash the streets to rid them of the blood of the demonstrators and their shoes and school bags were collected to prepare the city ready for the coming day. But people could see the bullet holes and bloody hand prints of wounded people on the street walls during the day.

    Polad's apartment was a good distance from my parent's house, but it never bothered us. We would jump in a cab to be together without a second thought. Besides, I had a car by this time and could drive there to see my fiancé anyway. I never attended any anti-government demonstrations with Polad or his friends. But I did get into numerous demonstrations on my own. I think I wasn't really suitably dressed for running in the streets and dodging the bullets, so every now and then I could see other girls' curious faces when I was passing by in the crowd.

I learned to burn cardboard near me to avoid my eyes burning from the tear gas. I learned to never ever separate from the crowd into a side road because the government paid people would follow you and God knows what they would do to you when you were alone. One day after being in street demonstrations for hours and having been hit on the upper back with a two by four by one of the guys, who was demonstrating for Shah's government, I decided to separate from everybody and go home.

As I turned into a side road the traffic light turned red and I was able to pass the intersection easily. I had a feeling that I was being followed and I turned to look behind me, and I saw a big guy with a red face coming towards me. In the few seconds that I looked at him I saw his eyes zooming in on me, as if I was a prey and he was a hunter. He had a very round face and square kind of body. With his short neck, small lips and narrow eyes, he looked like the Iranians who are from Turkmenistan.

There was something horrible about that face that I will never forget. I went among the standing cars and he followed exactly the way I moved. I looked at some of the people in the cars, but nobody wanted to get involved. I changed my route several times and he followed exactly with the same pattern. I knew he was after me so I started walking in between the cars and caused a huge traffic tangle.

Suddenly I saw a house with a half open door so I ran into that house and shut the door behind me! I had no idea whose house it was and what kind of people were living there, but I had to get away from that guy and I did! I was so scared that I could hear my heart beating in my throat. I felt an urge to go to the bathroom, but I had to control myself to wait to get home. I was standing in the yard with my hands still on the door and my back towards the building.

I heard some movement behind me and I turned like a wild animal in a cage. It was an old woman holding her Chador (Islamic cover) under her chin walking towards me. She said: "Come in and stay for ten minutes or so; they will have passed the street by then." I don't know if she thought I was running away from demonstrators or if she knew what was going on, but I decided not to elaborate. I thanked her and sat on the inside steps for a while. When I finally opened the yard door the street was quiet and I couldn't see that guy, so I jumped into a cab and went home.

Once I was over at Polad's apartment for the whole day and as I was getting ready to come home we realized that it was already dark and being in the streets wouldn't be safe for me. He wanted me to stay, but I had to be home every night regardless! Staying out for the night was not an option even though we were engaged. Polad offered to walk me to my car, but we both decided that it was a bad idea for him to walk back to his apartment after that.

As I left his building and started quickly walking towards the back ally where I had parked my car I realized that there was no sound in the street, except the clickety clack sound of my high heels echoing so loud. I could see my car in the dark, but I had a few more feet to reach it. I sensed a movement on my right across the street and looked up. There was one of the Shah's soldiers down on one knee aiming his rifle towards me. There was another one standing next to him smoking a cigarette while he was staring at me. In a glance I saw his face as he inhaled the smoke from his cigarette; he was not a young kid.

I guess, as he watched me walking, he was convinced that someone dressed like me, hurriedly tottering along, in high heels towards a parked car couldn't be one of the revolutionary people. They stood there motionless until I got in my car. As I drove away my heart was pounding in my throat and my hands were shaking so badly that changing the gear from one to two seemed to be an extremely difficult task that night!

On another occasion, as Polad was driving my car and I was the passenger, we got stuck in Tehran's traffic. It was one of our famous hot summer days and we were painfully inching along at a snail's pace. Tehran was changing; people were changing and Shah's men were putting more pressure on people who looked or acted suspicious. I was really hot in the slow-moving car and we didn't, of course, have air conditioning in our cars back then. I had my window rolled down to let some air in. Polad told me to roll the window back up,

I asked: "Why? It is hot you know!" He became angry and ordered me to do so. As we were arguing, a white sedan with four big guys in it began crawling up very close to us from Polad's side. The white cars with big guys as passengers were known to be the Shah's secret agents, known as "SAVAK" guys. They began saying things to provoke Polad, so he stopped the car and got out to see what exactly they wanted! He should never have done that, but he did. He didn't have his jeans and sneakers on. I think we were on our way to a family event because he was all dressed up with slacks and party shoes.

As he approached their car, all four guys descended from their car! He threw a punch at one guy, hitting him directly on the nose, and as he tried to kick another one he slipped with those shoes. As he was coming down on the hot asphalt they all gathered around, and each man held one arm or leg so that one of them could kick him in the stomach as he was spread wide open on the ground.

There was no time to "think"; I jumped in the driver's seat and drove directly towards them. They saw me coming, but didn't believe that I would actually hit them. When they saw that I was not slowing down, they dropped him directly in front of my car. I hit the brakes and stopped the car as one of the front tires rolled on his hand. They were looking at me as if I had horns or something and one of them said to him: "Go home; you have a woman with you." Another one screamed: "His hand, his hand; you are on his hand!" I slowly moved the car back a few inches and as he was getting up I heard him say: "That's not a woman; that's a tiger," and he got in the car.

If I remember rightly, during the three months of our engagement we broke up at least two times. We were constantly fighting, but didn't work out that our marriage wasn't exactly the smartest move on our part. The truth was that I had nothing in common with him or his circle of friends. No matter how much I was trying, I knew in my heart that I was different.

Sometimes when I look back I feel bad for Polad too. The poor guy had to keep his friends with me at his side and it couldn't have been easy. His buddies were all well-read working class guys and their girlfriends or wives were sweet, quiet people who didn't believe in makeup or wearing any jewelry. Among all of them there was one couple that I could relate to, but the wife and I never developed a close friendship. There were writers, artists and film makers among his friends, but with the same outlook towards the world and wealth.

We did both make an effort, in our own way, as our hiking trip may illustrate. In hindsight, it probably also illustrates how Polad and I were a lost cause...

The Hiking Trip-Summer of 1978

The summer of our engagement we decided to go on a long trip to see some of the moving tribes of Iran. They were groups of people who weren't allowed to stay in one area during the year. The Shah's government was afraid of these tribes uniting, so they used to be forced to move all the time. Our group consisted of three couples and one single guy. One couple was married; we were engaged and the other two were just boyfriend and girlfriend.

Polad was skeptical at first to take me with him on that trip. He explained that those people were well trained in hiking, and taking me along could have slowed them down. I was able to convince him that I would be strong and quiet and wouldn't be any cause of embarrassment for him. One night we all gathered together and checked the backpacks for some minimal clothing, dried bread, some canned foods, fire making needs, gas lanterns, one medium frying pan, water containers and blankets. Each person was supposed to have a backpack not heavier than fifty pounds. We took the train to the last station in the North West of Iran and started to walk from there.

I was a high heel gal and didn't even own a pair of hiking boots! I remember packing the night before; as I was looking for a suitable pair of shoes, I found an old pair of hiking boots that were one size too small for me. Since I had no idea what I was about to endure, I grabbed them and started the trip wearing boots that were too small for me. The first few hours of walking was tiring and after that it was a matter of tolerating the pain in my toes and back, and just staring at the feet ahead of me, which were going up and coming down, going up again and coming down.

I kept to my promise and just walked without a word until I opened my eyes and Polad was trying to feed me some bread and bean soup. I have no idea how far we had walked or what had happened. All I know is that I heard him say: "We need to rest here; the girls can't continue anymore." I heard Nader's wife, Susan say: "*The girls* are fine…let's go further…" but Polad convinced them to stop and rest for that night. We got up early in the morning and after having a small amount of food started to walk again. Polad was right; these people could walk for days without complaining, and I was almost dying trying to keep up with them.

We finally arrived at the spot that they had in mind and camped out. It was so beautiful that I forgot about my toes and lower back pain. A large green forest spread out behind our tents and a line of mountains lay behind that. In front was a wide river with large rocks in the water. There were some flowering shrubs that I had never seen before. They were very tall with large dark red flowers on top. The clean air smelt like fresh cut grass mixed with burned wood. We spent two nights in that spot. It was fun sitting around the fire and mixing cans of beans, tuna and noodles for dinner and calling it Mexican Cousin.

The sky was so bright with stars that you would think you could reach out and touch them. The only problem was that the side towards the fire would feel as if you were burning and the other side was as cold as ice. So we would change sides to warm up our other sides. We had two tents, one for the girls and one for the guys. The tents were rather small, so I talked to the girls and we decided to keep our backpacks outside of our tent to make more room for our sleeping bags.

Before I realized what was happening, Polad came towards me and ordered me to immediately put the backpacks inside the tent. I told him that it was silly to make the tent even smaller by taking up the space with three backpacks, but he wouldn't give me a moment to finish my sentence. He raised his voice and instructed me to follow his orders. I was so humiliated and upset, but had no other choice than to put them inside the tent. I walked away from the group and tried to cool off by looking at the view.

Later on, he walked towards me and as he sat down next to me, said:

"They say you are upset with me; is that true?" I looked at him trying so hard to remain civilized, saying:

"Yes, I am," and I reminded him about the backpacks and the tent. He looked at me and said:

"Well, you see, you don't understand my reasons, but I know what I'm doing." After I asked him to explain, he said:

"You girls have personal items in your backpacks and the guys may go through them and look at them."

I couldn't believe the nonsense he was telling me. First of all, what did it matter if they did look at my underwear and bra? Secondly, these were his buddies we were talking about. If he didn't trust them, why was he traveling with them? But I knew not to say any of that because it would have begun a huge fight and it wouldn't be good to embarrass myself or him in front of his friends.

Finally, we arrived at the tribe's camp. There were black tents made of goat's wool all across the horizon. All the women were carrying their babies wrapped on their backs and all the men were carrying rifles. They all had sun tanned dark skins. The women had straight soft black hair that was partially covered on top with a head band decorated with coins and beads at the edges. They all had narrow noses and beautiful large eyes and some of them even had green or blue eyes. Many of them had blue tattoos on their face and hands.

Their first question asked was if there were women among our group, and afterwards their second question was: "Where are your kids?" Most of their children looked sick. The adults had rotten teeth and the kids' faces seemed to be swollen on one side or both. They gathered around us showing their teeth and wounds asking for help. They mistakenly thought we were a medical group who were there to help them. It was very sad that we had no way of helping these people. One of them asked for the empty cooking oil container that we were using, to carry drinking water in so we gave it to him.

They invited us to have some rich goat milk and thick yogurt with them. We were sitting on a hill looking down at the wild river. The black tents were spread out, but yet in an almost circular formation. The air was full of the odor of goats and burned wood. I thought maybe having some yogurt wouldn't hurt my stomach. As I knew they used the river for bathing, washing the goats and their drinking water, I was trying to be careful with what I was eating and drinking there.

After a day or so we started hiking back towards the train station and on this trek I was progressing much better than when we started…until I felt the need to use a corner of the field as a bathroom every ten minutes, that is! I wasn't the only victim of diarrhea -- one other girl was experiencing the same inconvenience.

We made it back home and the wedding was in about 3 weeks. I was well trimmed after the twelve days of hiking and my dark skin was even darker. My mother wasn't very happy about that.

The Wedding -- September 1978

During that summer our relatives from the US and Europe came back to Tehran to attend our engagement party, or wedding, or both. It was customary for a lot of families to send their high school graduate children to the US or European countries for their college education. Polad's sister and her husband came back from New York, Polad and I were supposed to collect them at the airport. We arrived there and were standing in the large waiting area, trying to hear the flight information announcements that were given in two or three languages.

As I was standing there looking into thin air and miles away in thought, I felt Polad's heavy breathing in my face. Just as I turned my face towards him to see what was happening, he grabbed my arm and dragged me out of the airport. He wouldn't say why and I still don't know his reason, but I suspect that he thought that I was flirting with a man with my eyes!

He was pulling me and I was trying really hard to keep my balance and walk normally. It was a horrible moment -- he was hurting my arm and I was humiliated in front of at least a couple of hundred people. He threw me out and I walked to my car, sobbing heavily.

That day I drove to his brother's house and explained to his mother, in a flood of tears, what had happened. Her reaction was that the men in that family had bad tempers and it was the women's job to keep them happy and not be offended by their language and acts. She explained to me that I should just ignore that kind of behavior and accept it easily. She assured me that Polad must have felt very sorry and regretful as soon as he had returned to the waiting area and realized that I wasn't there with him(?!)

A few days later I went back to his brother's house to meet his sister and her husband. They were nice people and had brought me a very pretty wedding gown from New York. All was set for the wedding now...

The original wedding date had to be postponed for a week due to a massacre of unarmed demonstrators by the Shah's army. That day has remained in the memory of the Iranian people as "Black Friday".

From the middle of 1978, street demonstrations had reached an unprecedented level. The Shah replaced Amuzegar with Sharif-Emami as the Prime Minister in August. He had been in that position before and had a reputation for being corrupt. In fact, he was known as 'Mr. Ten Percent', as it was believed that he had taken ten percent of government funds for himself. So, not really a good decision on the Shah's part!

At this time many cities were placed under martial law, to curb the demonstrations, but it was too late. People poured into the streets to defy the Shah. It was no longer just the middle classes demonstrating; the working classes, who had been losing their jobs, were joining the ranks of the demonstrators too. Sharif-Emami sent the army in front of the people. This time tanks were used to disperse the demonstrators. This tactic was unsuccessful.

The soldiers were ordered to shoot, and according to the opposition, more than six hundred people were killed in Zhaleh Square alone. This day, September 8th, became known as 'Black Friday' and the name of the square was changed to the 'Square of Martyrs'. Since the debut of his appointment Sharif-Emami had tried to reach a kind of compromise with the moderate groups of the opposition, but Black Friday made any compromise impossible. The Shah, once more, changed the Prime Minister. This time, in November, he appointed General Azhari , a military man. It was useless. The country became paralyzed by the daily demonstrations and workers' strikes in major industries, including the oil industry.

This picture shows us walking through the door into our yard.

Back to our wedding… Due to the country's circumstances, the wedding plan became much simpler than the engagement party. We invited about fifty people to our house for the ceremony, and after that about forty people drove with us to Polad's brother's house for a short reception.

Nothing new happened between us after the wedding. We fought like angry dogs and he was still very harsh with me. Once I asked him: "If you feel like this about me, why did you marry me?" He answered: "I didn't want to release a wrong deed in society".

At the time I didn't understand what he meant and it took me years to actually get it. He was telling me that as we had been together for many years and I was known to be his girl-friend, he did me a favor by marrying me, so that I wouldn't bring shame on my family or myself.

Well, it wouldn't have given me any bad reputation what so ever because my family would have insisted on sending me to the US, to live with my brother and go to college there. Now, I am asking myself why I married Polad. I think it was for the same reason. I wanted to tell my father that I was a good girl and I hadn't tarnished his name and also, I was feeling very sorry for Polad. I had learned in my life to care for others before "me" and I couldn't leave him alone to live the life that he had created for himself.

Sometimes I think maybe if I had been more mature I could have prevented some of our arguments from getting to the point of him beating me. We were both very young and he had a lot of anger in him. I was as bad when we got into an argument. I would verbally carry on with insults and screams too. There is no excuse for domestic abuse, but my attitude may not have helped either. If I could turn back the time, knowing what I know today, I would still make the same decision. I would choose to marry Polad and have my two beautiful children.

One of Polad's sisters, who had travelled from the US to Tehran for our wedding, worked for an international airline. She wanted so badly to send us on a honeymoon trip. She called me at my father's house a few days before our wedding to discuss that with me. She was willing to accept the entire trip's expenses and I said "No"! She was completely confused and wanted to understand why I wouldn't want to go away for free with my husband. I explained to her:

"I really appreciate what you want to do for us, but I don't think it would be a good idea." When she asked why, I told her:

"Because Polad and I always get into terrible fights when we are alone, and especially if, God forbid, some guy looks at me…it would be a horrible time for both of us." She accepted my explanation and said no more on the subject.

###

We had rented a small clean second floor apartment from an elderly couple who were living with their oldest daughter in Tehran. It is customary in Iran that the bride goes to her new home with a complete set of furniture and dishes that she and her husband will need to have a comfortable life. They call this the Bride's "Jaheezieh" (dowry). My father had paid and my mother had purchased me a complete set of bedroom, living room, and dining room furniture, a complete kitchen including washer, dryer, stove, a set of China and a set of silverware for twelve people, plus a large handmade Persian rug.

The wedding was wrapped up pretty fast and everybody was eager to get home as soon as possible, to avoid any problems with the police and army, who had all the roads under surveillance. We went home around 8p.m. and started our new life together as husband and wife.

Nothing had changed regarding our social network. There were his friends whom we were hanging out with and sometimes my sister and parents. I remember that I asked my mom to come over one night for a bite to eat and I was stunned when I opened the door and saw her dressed up wearing all of her fine jewelry!

My parents came in and sat down acting as if they were formal guests! I had seen other young bride's moms who would just go to their daughter's house in their sport shoes and comfortable clothing to talk and go shopping together. I had seen mothers who would go to their daughter's kitchen and start helping without hesitation, so I really didn't know how to handle my mom. It took me a few years to realize that she was so lonely and wrapped up in her bad marriage that she couldn't even think about having a relationship with her grown daughter.

Mom had no friends and no place to go and that was the reason for her dressing up and coming to my house. I also knew that my mom was not really a traditional mom; she was a career woman who had always worked as a school teacher and went to the hair dresser twice a week, no matter what. I knew well that she wouldn't be the type to be a grandma to my children, letting me leave my baby with her for a few hours. Anyway, that gathering was repeated probably one more time during my marriage and no more.

Once we were married, Polad's older brother suggested for the whole family to drive to a beautiful vacation resort at the Caspian Sea. He knew of the resort through the large international company where he worked. We all got together with his brothers, sisters, mom and grandma and drove three cars to the seaside. It was a beautiful resort with swimming pools, waterfalls and many apartments and condos. There were large heart shaped signs and even paintings on the road showing directions to the different buildings and activities.

Apparently, before Iran started going through the turmoil of the revolution, that resort was the place for wealthy Iranians and foreigners to enjoy a very free and glamorous life-style during their vacations. It was at the end of summer when we went there, the end of September, and due to the extreme changes in Iran's society the resort was empty and quiet.

Polad's brother had arranged for us to have one of the apartments for a few nights and we would drive to the nearest town for food shopping to prepare a meal in the apartment. One evening Polad's brother and wife left their kids with the others and just the four of us went out to dinner. The first night the family offered Polad and I an outside bed with a see through mosquito net and the others slept inside. Polad's little nephew wanted so badly to sleep with us, so the little boy slept in our bed and I think that saved our lives that night.

As always Polad was in his own world about what was the right thing to do, and I was in mine. I wanted him to lock the car doors at night and park it near the building, right next to our outside bed. He argued with me that nobody was there and the resort was gate protected. We were sleeping and the dark night was getting a bit lighter as the day was rising up in the sky. I have always been a very light sleeper; that very early morning, with my eyes still closed, I heard a sound as if a dog was walking on the asphalt and his claws were making the noise.

Then I heard very heavy breathing next to my head from outside of the mosquito net. I thought that it must be a hungry stray dog and that it would be better if I didn't acknowledge its presence, so it would go away. Hence, I didn't even open my eyes. Polad heard something too and whispered: "What is that noise?" I said that it was probably a dog and we went back to sleep. A few hours later we woke up to find out that someone had gone through the car and stolen some items, including Polad's large hunting knife. There is no doubt in my mind that the locals, who had always seen that place to be occupied by men and women who weren't married, came to check us out, and if it hadn't been for the little boy who was sleeping in our bed, we would have been killed that night.

Chapter Six

Married Life

I felt like the queen of my castle when we started our lives together in that apartment. It was *my* beautiful home and I was in charge inside those walls, just as all the women in my family were in charge of their homes. But that really didn't help much when our marriage was always on the rocks. One night at about 7 p.m. after my evening class, when I got in my car to drive home, I realized that something was wrong with the car; the lights didn't have much power and the car was slowly dying on me. I quickly realized that the car battery was not getting charged, so I turned off the radio and the lights and drove home in the dark praying that I would make it home safe and sound.

There were no cell phones back then and due to the political situations in Iran, the streets weren't safe after dark. I arrived home an hour late. I was so happy that I had made it home! I parked the car, grabbed my books and ran up the steps towards our apartment door. As soon as I put my hand on the door knob Polad opened it from the inside; without saying a word, he grabbed me by my clothing and pulled me inside. He was hitting me non-stop, with punches and slaps -- without asking why I was late…

Later on he said that that one hour was the most devastating hour of his life up to that day. He was worried sick not knowing what had happened to me. Well, he certainly could have told me that when I arrived instead of doing what he did. It was so bad that our landlord's wife came up to our apartment and took him downstairs to their place. Have I mentioned that Polad was a very strong man who had been a wrestler a few years back?

That night, among all the insults that he fired at me, he claimed that he had called my mother and "let her have it". I had to call my mother to see how she was doing, so I pulled myself together and sat on the edge of our bed, picked up the phone and dialed my old number. Suddenly, I felt the phone cord being wrapped around my neck. It took me a few seconds to understand that I had to defend myself… I grabbed the old heavy telephone unit and hit him in his face which was looming over my head. I got up as soon as the cord became loose and witnessed him turning around on one foot and falling down, in a very theatrical manner, onto the floor.

I calmly took a long stride over his body and went to the kitchen. After a few minutes he got up and walked to join me in the kitchen, looking at me as if I had committed a crime; then he turned around and walked away...

I slept on the kitchen floor that night and moved to my bed in the morning after he had left the house. My whole body was aching. He had held me by my hair the night before so my scalp was sore too. I was so tired and couldn't get up. I had planned to leave the bed before he returned home, but I couldn't. I slept another night and the next day and the day after... I would wake up and realize that I had wet the bed, but I had no energy to get up to change the sheets. The pillow was covered with some of my hair that had come out and I couldn't keep awake long enough to even eat or drink. On the third morning I opened my eyes and saw a worried Polad standing over my side of the bed staring at me; he pointed to some hard boiled eggs on the side table and said: "You need to eat something." I closed my eyes again and he left... I finally went back to my classes, but as I had a purple eye, I had to use purple eye-shadow for a while on both eyes, as camouflage.

Something similar happened again. I can't remember all the details or what it was about. Maybe it was about me smoking cigarettes (he was a smoker too, but didn't like me doing it). I'm not sure, but this time I really thought I had to get out of that life. I remember the fight. He hit me and I threw a crystal ashtray at him – it missed; then I threw a large round wooden chopping board at him which hit the wall and broke in two. I almost grabbed the propane tank to throw at him, but I stopped myself...

He left and I was sitting on the steps inside the hallway crying. I was crying for all that I had gambled and lost in marrying him. I was crying for all the names that he used to call me, so comfortably, as if I really WAS a prostitute. I was devastated... I couldn't go back home after what I had put my parents through to agree to our marriage. I truly decided that there was no reason and no place for me to live any more.

Suddenly, I wasn't sad anymore -- as always, I had found a way "out". It seemed very justified; I had no children, my family had been torn apart a long time ago, and I had no tight connection to either one of them. I thought about my mother, but as they say, "You never know the feeling until you become a mother yourself". So I thought she would be sad, but she would get over it... "Besides," I thought to myself, "she will still have her first born and her baby."

I took a heap of sleeping pills and any other pills that I could find in our apartment. As I was sitting calmly waiting for the end, I thought: "What if he comes back and after seeing me like this hits me again?" I hurriedly left the apartment and began driving towards the highway. I stopped to see a friend; she wasn't there, so I continued driving. My eyes were getting tired and a relaxing, comfortable feeling of deep sleep was coming over me... I realized that I shouldn't be driving. I realized that I could cause other people's deaths or severe injuries simply because I was too selfish to stay at home and possibly receive my last beating.

I turned around and made it back home, parked the car at a funny angle and stumbled inside. He was there, standing before me and looking at me with those big angry black eyes. He grabbed my arm as he asked: "What did you take? Huh? Answer me; what did you take?"

It felt like a few minutes before I could answer, but finally the name of the sleeping pill passed between my lips, as my eyes were getting warmer, heavy...and closed. It felt so good and comfortable. I was about to be free -- no pain, no beatings, no hurtful words, no more worrying.

I remember being pulled towards the door and helped down the stairs. We were in the car and I put my head back and closed my eyes. I could hear him talking from a distance, as if his voice was coming from across a large room, I could feel the car moving like a baby carriage and it was soothing.

As soon as we walked through the ER, I heard two nurses whispering to one another: "She took pills"... The doctor came in... I would be woken up by them shaking me and asking questions... Later, we were in a big dim room with many beds. I woke up when they handed me a bucket of salt water to drink... I woke up again when the bucket was on the floor and an old man was mopping up; he looked at me and shook his head, blaming me with his eyes... I woke up again when a doctor was screaming in my face and shaking my shoulders... He said: "There is a little blood above your lip."
I said: "I know" and went back to sleep... It felt so good and I just didn't want to come back. They couldn't understand it.

I couldn't understand all of that nervousness, screaming and shaking. I woke up again, turned my face to the right, and there was a woman in a hospital gown walking around with the metal pole with an IV hanging from it. She looked lost and far away. She turned around and walked away from me. By that time I had thrown up a few times, but just wanted to sleep.

Another doctor came around to the side of that cold metal bed, with no mattress; he told Polad:
"Take her out of here; these people are all mental patients."

We had been there for a few hours and when I walked out, leaning on Polad's shoulders, I saw my parents in the parking lot. Polad had a big bag of juice bottles in his hand. I looked at my parents and sat in the car. They didn't look terribly worried, but my father's eyes were darker than usual, Polad drove us away and I saw my parents standing there, gradually becoming smaller as we got further and further away. Later on, he said that he had told my parents that I had food poisoning.

Chapter Seven
Changes – Living with a Revolutionist

When we got married I still had one more year of college ahead of me. I was going to college and taking care of our little apartment. It was small and looked beautiful with cherry color wood furniture that had light blue velvet fabric. A few months after our marriage the revolution took place in Iran (February through April of 1979), and soon everything started to change. Life was no longer about revolution and freedom. It was about Islam and obeying the Islamic government rules. People were changing and were taking sides, so I wasn't very fond of my old circle of friends any longer either. During the few months between our wedding and the revolution many things had also changed in my family. My sister had broken off her engagement with her fiancé and had left Iran for Italy. My mother joined her after a short while.

###

My last year of college was very different from the previous three years. I became very close to a friend whose mother was also one of my mom's old best friends! Ironically, we ended up in the same college and became best friends. My friend, Shirin was one of the most amazing people that I had ever met in my life; she was tall, beautiful, down to earth and very innocent. Polad never liked any of my friends and wanted me to distance myself from Shirin too, but I fought back and continued my friendship with her. We used to sit in her room and talk, laugh and talk more for hours. I couldn't write about any of my problems to my own family and couldn't trust any other friend either. Shirin became my mom, my sister and my best friend. Soon after our graduation from college she decided to leave Iran for Europe, to see the world and continue to grow. So we were separated and each went along our own path in life…
(We reunited in 2011 in California, USA)

###

During the revolution period, a lot of people were shot in the streets of Tehran and other large cities in Iran. I had heard an estimate of seventy thousand people back then, but I'm not sure if this is accurate or not. Hearing the explosions and bullet shots became part of normal daily life for a lot of us. I remember, one day I was hanging out our washed bedsheets, on the line on our balcony, and I could hear the bullet sounds from far off. Suddenly, I started to hear a different sound after each shot. It was like an extended "shshsh" noise and there they were -- golden hot pointed bullets landing right on my balcony, next to my feet! I immediately dropped down on the ground, crawled into the room and stayed away from the windows until the shooting had stopped that day.

After one year living in our apartment, Polad and I moved to my parent's house. I was under the impression that maybe we couldn't afford to pay the rent any longer. Although my parents were still living there, our home was large enough for us to live there too. Their bedroom was on the second floor and the rest of the house was fully furnished with no residents. At first, Polad and I took the living room on the first floor which was next to the kitchen, and as always, my father provided the food and paid all the bills without bringing up those subjects with us. My sister had left Iran for Italy a while back, and in her letters to us she revealed her dissatisfaction with living there by herself. The goal from the beginning was for her to go to the US, to our brother; so my mom left Iran for Italy, to help her through getting the visa for the US.

Now that my mom was gone, my father, who was still living on the second floor all by himself, became totally free to go wherever he wished whenever he wished.

###

Almost immediately after the revolution, Iraq and Iran were at war. The new Islamic government demanded people's birth certificates to enable them to issue families with provision coupons. We needed coupons for everything including meat, rice, cooking oil, butter, soap, eggs and much more. This was, of course, also a good opportunity for the Islamic government to get all the information that they needed from people all over the country. Everybody needed food to survive; therefore, everybody had to tell the "Local Islamic Committees" about who they were and where they were living!

###

One of my mother's older sisters was a very sweet, religious woman who had been married for forty years without being able to have any children. I've already mentioned her to you -- her name was Auntie Nour. "Nour" means light in Farsi and she was as delightful and innocent as the rays of the sun.

Auntie Nour was very different from her other sisters. She always had a smile on her face; she was a small, fast moving and energetic person. She loved children so much that she became a Baha'i school teacher. A session was held once a week in someone's home. Among all of our relatives she was the only one who brought a dog to her house and treated it like her child, something that we all do nowadays, but wasn't very common in Iran back in those years.

Nour was fair skinned; her skin was so sensitive that even plasters would leave a line of rash. She loved cooking, baking and sewing for her home and the neighborhood. I remember that she was loved by everybody, and people regardless of their religion would come to see her. She was also a sort of marriage counselor for her friends and neighbors. Once, when I was visiting her, a woman came over and complained about her husband who was not paying her any attention any more. Auntie Nour talked to her a little and then told her to buy some low price fabric so she could make her a few new dresses. She also gave her some tips on airing the house after cooking to have a fresh smelling home, and to always look presentable for her husband, no matter how tired she might be.

Auntie Nour and her husband used to live in a small house very near to our home, but eventually we all moved away from that area and they moved to a suburb of Tehran. As I have mentioned, Auntie Nour was very religious, but not narrow-minded at all. Ever since I had my car I would visit her sometimes. One day when I was there she told me to walk to the store with her, so we left the house together. She said jokingly:
"If anybody asks who you are, we are going to tell them that you are my daughter who has been in the UK for years and is just visiting us!"
We laughed heartily, but right there and then, I realized how much she must have prayed to become a mother, and I felt so bad for her. As we were walking, I put my arm around her and said:
"Auntie Nour, you are like a mom to me and all of your nieces, and we love you like a mom." She smiled and looked at me with loving eyes.

As the Islamic government in Iran was getting established, almost immediately they started to capture different groups of the population as "traitors of the Islamic Republic of Iran". At the time of the revolution, all the different groups of people, including those who believed in a western republican government, those who were followers of the Chinese communist party (Mao), those who were following the Soviet communist party, those who believed in a free Islamic country and the Islamic fanatic party who believed in Khomeini, had all put their differences aside and fought against the Shah's regime as one group.

For one week we had a real free Iran and as soon as Khomeini came to power everything turned upside down. We would stare at our television sets or listen closely to the radios with confused faces. What just happened? Who voted for him to be our leader? We didn't turn our country into a war zone for *these people* to take control…but it was too late. It seemed that the western big brothers had been planning this for decades, to create fanatic Islamic governments in all Middle Eastern countries, in order to firstly stop the Soviet Union's influence in the area and secondly, to stop the populations of these countries from growing mentally (due to the nature of religion in general), so that the big brothers could get to the oil in the Middle East more easily.

As the Islamic government started capturing, kidnapping and killing people, the Baha'i followers became a target again. Auntie Nour and her husband were in clear danger in their little town, but they wouldn't move away. As I recall, she had told my other aunt that if God needed them to be saved he would bring it about, and if God needed more blood to nourish the Baha'i faith, then they had to stay. One day, I received the news that Auntie Nour and her husband had been captured in their home during a midnight raid by Islamic solders known as "Pasdars". The following is what we heard from the neighbors.

At around 2 a.m. a large group of Pasdars surrounded their house at both the front door and the walls around their yard. They broke the front door down to get in. They were inside searching and taking valuables and breaking whatever they could, just to instill fear in them, until the dawn and then they took my aunt and her husband to the back porch. It is said that my aunt's husband asked the intruders:

"At least let me free the dog out of the house so when we are gone he won't die of hunger." One of them replied:

"You want me to free your dog? Here, he is free now," and he shot the beautiful Cocker Spaniel in the head. Just this moment in the event must have been extremely devastating for this quiet and gentle couple who were over 65 years old…

The Islamic government wanted the captured Baha'i members to sign a confession that their religion was a made-up foreign tactic and that they wanted to become Muslims. At the time, they had almost five hundred people in jail and under torture for the same reason. After a few years of torturing them they executed my aunt and her husband, and took over their house and all of their possessions, including their retirement bank account.

During that time I couldn't pay them a visit in jail. It hurt so badly that I couldn't visit Nour. I thought about her constantly. I wanted Nour to see my baby bump. When Auntie Parie said that Nour needed clothes, I sent some of Mom's clothes, knowing that she would recognize them. She sent a message back saying that she thanked all her nieces and knew that they wanted to visit her, but it was okay; she loved them... She had understood that I was thinking of her. I knew that the authorities would look into all visitors' backgrounds and I wouldn't do anything to jeopardize Polad's safety.

Auntie Nour was an angel who was always singing and smiling, with a wonderful sense of humor. She didn't deserve this outcome done in the name of religion.

My other aunt, Parie, who was the youngest, had gone to the usual jail to visit Nour. She was told that Nour was no longer there; she had been transferred to another jail. Parie was sent from one place to another until finally, she discovered the truth – her sister had been executed. She stepped forward and claimed their bodies. The body of Nour was delivered in a large plastic bag. Although the local neighborhood store owners -- the butcher, the carpenter, the traders Auntie Nour had dealt with over the years -- were Muslims, and not Baha'i, they gathered together to provide ice, to prevent the body from rotting, saying that she was such a wonderful woman and they were a good family...

I couldn't even participate in their funeral. It hurt me so much that I couldn't visit Nour while she was in jail, and now I couldn't say farewell at her funeral. I remember having a dream about my aunt a few days later. In my dream she was wearing a checkered winter coat which I had seen her wearing before. When she took off her coat, I saw that her upper back was black and blue. I called my other aunt when I woke up and begged her to tell me about her sister's body after she collected it from the Islamic government. She told me that my aunt had a burn mark, in the shape of a household iron, on her upper back and the body didn't have much blood on it while they were washing it for burial. She added that it appeared that they had killed her during torture and shot her after death to pretend that she had been executed.

At the time I was six months pregnant with my first child... It was a devastating blow to me... Dear Auntie Nour, killed in the name of religion and I repeat – in the name of religion – not in the name of God (for no loving God would want his creations, which were created out of love, to suffer in this way). If nothing else, it isn't logical. Auntie Nour was killed out of Man's greed...with false accusations of being a traitor. She was a traitor to no one and no thing.

I am angry...I am angry with the Baha'i, as well as the Islamic religious organizations...I am angry at any controlling organization. I feel bitter towards the Baha'i organization. Their headquarters is in Haifa, Israel. They have funds, or could gather together funds from their rich members. They could send money and aid to help their members, but the blood of the martyrs watering the meadows of Iran is promotion for the Baha'i organization, is it not?

That bothers me a great deal. When you are a leader of a flock, you have a responsibility to protect that flock. You would expect them to pull these people out from their suffering. But no! At the time, the Baha'i HQ had announced that no Baha'i should leave Iran. Nour and her husband would not have gone anyway; they were ready to die for their beliefs. They had known that their address was under surveillance and the phone line was being tapped, and had spoken in coded conversations. They wanted to be martyrs for their religion.

Although I am bitter towards the Baha'i religion, I still took my children to the Baha'i school in the US. The school was quite a long way away and I couldn't afford the gas to return home, so I would sleep in the car while they were in school. It was that important to me. Why? Because their faith is based on the basics of humanity, believing in all religions and all prophets who come to guide God's flock. Baha'i teaching is wonderful -- don't hurt anyone; don't do what you wouldn't want done to you; don't touch what belongs to others without asking permission -- but I hadn't been an active Baha'i. I went to the school, but stopped practicing once I left and didn't promote the religion.

I was actually exiled from the Baha'i religion when I arrived in the US. I rang the Baha'i Centre in Chicago to request my Baha'i ID card, and was informed that I no longer belonged to that flock. I had committed the terrible sin of leaving Iran, against their orders to stay, along with the other "martyrs". The Baha'i organization wanted members to add their blood to the advertising, not leave and escape the suffering and death. I told the man at the center to return to Iran with his wife and family, so that they could all add their blood. He wasn't impressed with my answer! I can't think why... Anyway, I received a letter stating that I had been kicked out. But I took my children to Baha'i school, none the less.

Thus, it is not the teachings that I feel bitterness towards -- it is the organization and the wannabes in the organization. There are active Baha'i members who go through all the motions, but it is an illusion. It's a façade...they don't live by the teachings in their everyday lives. Neither do many practice what they preach!

Chapter Eight
Wonderful News

March 1981

We invited my dad out to dinner as soon as we found out about my pregnancy. There was a famous restaurant in Tehran of which my sister and I have many fond memories, so we invited my father to my all-time favorite restaurant "Joujeh Kababy Hatam".

While we were there, we informed him that he was about to become a grandfather for the first time. I thought he would be ecstatic, brimming over with joy, but boy was I wrong! Apparently, I was supposed to hide my pregnancy and be bashful about it. I had no idea that my dad was that fanatic. It was a very big deal for us to have a child together. My first pregnancy was a very bad experience. I had told Polad that I was pregnant and he gave me a list of demands that I *must* follow after having the baby. The list was about how the child would be raised, where I had to raise him/her and what sort of philosophy I was supposed to follow in raising our child!

For whatever reason, I miscarried that baby and it took us another two years to be able to conceive another child. I became ill with some infections and was told that I would never become pregnant again, so it *really* was a big deal for us to know that we were able to become parents.

My father was always on the go. He would either be in the US visiting my sister, brother and our mom, or going about his private life with *that other woman*. During my pregnancy I had nobody with whom to share my fears and hopes. I had a very small folded booklet that had pictures of the fetus in the womb at the different months of pregnancy. I used to look at those small colorful pictures every day to imagine how my unborn child would look inside me. There was no ultra-sound for expecting mothers back then, but I would visit my doctor once a month to make sure that the baby was doing well.

I sent this picture of me expecting Amir to my mom in the US back in 1981

During my pregnancy, Polad and his friends worked together to paint and carpet the whole house so we could move to the second floor, and my dad could change place with us on the first floor. Every night we had at least five people coming in after their daily jobs of being school teachers, college professors, artists...to paint the house and move the heavy furniture around. I would cook large meals for everyone and never wondered where all of that food was coming from! Polad paid for the house remodeling, but the food expenses were being paid for by my dad.

While I was getting heavier every day, I began emptying the closets of all the bedrooms that had been left half full for years. It wasn't emotionally easy to go back through my childhood without having my mother and sister present. When I opened my sister's old closet and found her clothing I cried so hard; I was feeling horrible that her clothing looked bad. Well, that was actually because she took the good and useful clothes with her to Europe, but at that moment it was really hard for me to see those clothes. We bagged everything for donating to the poor and brought my father's whole bedroom suite to the first floor. The work wasn't completely finished when I had to go to the hospital to give birth to our first child, but Polad and his friends took care of the rest during the twenty-four hours that I was in the hospital. I had been in pain all night, not knowing that it was *"the contraction pains"*. Finally, around 7 a.m. Polad took me to the hospital.

As my mother had instructed me when I was a teenager, I had had my hospital bag packed and ready since the seventh month of my pregnancy, so we just grabbed it and drove to the hospital. When we arrived, they sent Polad to the registration and told me to wait for him in the lobby behind the large door to the surgery department.

I was there and the pain was running through my body every few minutes. A woman about 40 years old approached me and asked where my mother was. I told her that she wasn't there, that she was abroad. So she asked for my mother-in-law or any other family member. I told her that I was alone with my husband, and he was downstairs at the registrations office. She screamed at a passing nurse and told her to take me inside immediately. The nurse replied that they MUST wait for my husband to come back with the paper work. The woman roared through her teeth:
"You will take her inside and give her a gown now or I will take her clothes off right here!"
Well, that worked and they took me inside, gave me a gown and guided me to the labor room. I never saw that lady again, but she was like an angel coming to my aid. Thank you, dear stranger.

The "labor room" was a large room with many beds in it. Each bed had curtains around it that could be closed (like in the ER). I was laying there with just one thought in my mind -- having my child in my arms and rushing back home where I would feel safe.

In between harsh contractions I could listen to the other women and one case seemed to be very strange and funny. Straight across from my bed there was a young heavy woman who didn't speak Farsi. She was from a Turkish speaking state -- most likely from Tabriz. She was screaming and finally a nurse came to her to see what was happening. After the nurse checked her out, I heard her tell the pregnant woman that she wasn't ready to have her baby yet and that she was only five or six months pregnant.

The Turkish lady couldn't understand the nurse and vice versa, so they used the hospital's paging system to bring a translator. The nurse repeated her sentence to the translator and the translator told the patient that she was only five or six months pregnant. The woman replied and the translator's face changed to sudden surprise. After a few seconds, trying very hard not to laugh, and pulling herself together, she said:
"Well, this woman says that she has come from a long way away and she cannot come back again -- just take care of the baby right now and hand it to her!"

On November 20th 1981, on a sunny Friday morning, Amir was born at 10:08 a.m. The birth was slightly complicated; the baby's head was very large and his whole body was bouncing back towards my chest after every push. My doctor wanted to perform a cesarean, but I knew we couldn't afford it; so I didn't give him permission and I managed to have my baby as a natural birth. He was a healthy little baby boy and Polad forgot all about his previous silly demands as soon as he saw his son in the nurse's arms! My dad gave us $50000 Rials for my hospital expenses.

Having Amir in my life changed my world. I was very focused on my baby and motherhood felt very natural to me. I wouldn't argue with

Polad anymore, and he was very respectful of my rights with our child. Although, in the past, he had rarely agreed with what I said or did, he was very supportive of my ways of mothering Amir. He left raising the child completely to me and I was very thankful for that. At last there was something that I could do without being criticized.

I was alone with no older female help and I think that had its advantages and disadvantages. It was nice that there was nobody to look over my shoulder and it was not so good when the baby was not feeling well. Amir was a very healthy and beautiful baby and I found a very nice older pediatrician who was very helpful. He would even write down soup recipes for me to make for the baby! Once he handed me a prescription and said:
"This is for you and not the baby." I looked at it and saw that he had written "Some patience and more sleep"! This doctor was recommended to us by other politically active young couples who had small children. Later on, I found out that he also had had a nephew in jail who was executed a few years later for political reasons.

It was the summer of 1982 when Polad asked me if we could invite some of his friends to my dad's shore house in North Iran. I asked my dad's permission and we arranged for about ten or so people to drive there, to stay for a few days and enjoy the weather and walk on the beach. We knew well, that nobody could go swimming due to the Islamic rules and the guys wouldn't even try to do it, just to avoid causing any curiosity in the area. Polad, me and 7 month old Amir drove to the shore house at night, and the others joined us in a few different cars during the night.

There were enough beds and everybody had brought their own blankets and bedding with them. All the women and children slept in one large room while all the guys were in another. We had large windows on both sides of that building, so by opening them we would get the cool breeze off the sea through the rooms with no need for air conditioning. It was fun and everybody was happy.

I noticed a young couple who would hold hands at every opportunity they could get. They looked older than the rest of us. I think he was probably 30 years old while we were mostly in our early twenties. Later on, I learned that the young man was a political prisoner during the previous government in Iran when the Shah was in power. He was apparently in jail for about seven or eight years and was released by people who rushed to the jails and let political prisoners out during the revolution back in 1979. He was originally from North West Iran and had never seen the sea in his life. This trip was for him to see the Caspian Sea for the first time. They had one little son and she was expecting another child at that time.

All of us would cook together and walk to the beach at sunset to play ball. People would take turns in holding the babies or keeping an eye on a few little children that we had among us. Fortunately, everything went well during that trip and we all came back to our homes with no incident.

Later on, I heard that the Islamic police had found the couple who were expecting their second child, after she had given birth to a little girl. I was told that when the Pasdars attacked their apartment, the husband stood on the window-sill and said that he had really lived during the past few years (from 1979 to 1983) and he would never go back to jail again. He told his wife and son that he loved them and jumped from the fourth floor down to his death on the sidewalk.

Chapter Nine
Challenges

After my little boy Amir came into our lives everything changed for me. I couldn't fight with my husband over every disagreement any more. I didn't want to shake the world around my little boy, so I became very passive and quiet with Polad. Polad wasn't very healthy either. He was an extremely passionate person in whatever he was doing, so you can imagine what his health would be like under all of that stress that he was experiencing every moment of the day. He was an active member of an anti-government organization which was losing members to torture and the death penalty every day.

At first, as he habitually didn't pay any attention to his body, Polad ignored the problem with his digestive system. One day he told me that his stomach was on fire. His face and eyes looked really dark. He told me that he hadn't been able to eat for a week, so I drove him to the emergency room. I had never seen him that fragile before; he was really sick and that broke my heart. They told him that he had a bleeding ulcer in his stomach, prescribed him some meds and gave some health advice and released him to come back home. He was to eat no spice and no fatty food, so I began cooking special meals for him, although it really wouldn't make much difference to his health, since he would be stressed out and still living that kind of life style.

One day he told me that a friend had given him some tips about how to deal with a bleeding ulcer. A friend had told a friend that he had heard it from someone in Russia -- drink half a glass of raw potato juice every morning on an empty stomach for twenty-one days. I started making it ready for Polad every morning and it did seem to help him. When I look back, I can't believe the life that we and all the other young people had during those years. I am very glad that I was neither interested nor forced by Polad to join his organization.

My life was a closed environment of a group of people of whom I wasn't really fond of. Sometimes one or two people would become a bit close to me for a short period of time and then go away by the force of our lifestyle and for security purposes. There was a young woman who became friends with me and started coming over when we were living at my dad's house. She was tall, with red hair and large green eyes. She was married to one of Polad's friends; her husband was in jail for his political activities and she had no family or friends to go to.

I think she came to our house one day with some other person and after that started visiting me and Amir every now and then. She had published a children's story book which was about a little spring that had a wish to see the world. The spring told the sun about its wish and the sun told it that the only way he could help was to evaporate the spring from its bed on the ground, and turn it into rain so it could see the entire world as it was coming down from the sky... What a beautiful story.

This young woman told me her story; they were originally from Gorgistan (Georgia) in the south of Russia. Her family had emigrated into Iran generations ago. She told me that her family was intertwined with the Shah's secret service, SAVAK and that was the way the SAVAK used to recruit -- the whole family would be involved to decrease the danger of agents losing their cover through other family members' curiosity. She showed me some marks of lashes on her body and said that her family tied her up and tortured her to know where her husband and his friends were hiding.

They also took pictures of her in that manner while she was tied up and beaten. She had run away to live a quiet life with her husband and became pregnant. They had a beautiful little girl and one day as she was standing at the doorway talking to the neighbors, an old man who was slowly backing his car out from his yard, bumped into their little child. After hitting her head on a rock she instantly died. Her husband was captured a few months later and here she was living in one room on the twelfth floor of a business building in the middle of Tehran.

I knew it wasn't really safe for Polad to let this woman into the house, but I felt so bad for her that I couldn't and wouldn't stop her from visiting us. Actually, I was really worried that she would commit suicide. I lost contact with her after we moved out of my dad's house and I never heard of her again. I hope she made it...

###

A major change in my life after I became a mother was that the thought of suicide totally left my mind. I loved taking care of my baby and I loved talking to him. I started talking calmly with Amir very early in his life. I would tell him about the different colors in an apple when you cut it and I would tell him how the little bird on the wire was trying to learn how to fly and how its parents were watching him from a distance. I always talked to him softly with a smile.

In Farsi there are two ways of addressing people with two different words for the word "you". One is formal as you refer to an older person or someone that you have just met and there is another word for referring to people in a more informal and close way. I don't really know why, but I talked to him using the formal word for "you" and it was so cute listening to him later on talking with others using the formal word!

Amir was a healthy cute baby boy

Amir was about 9 months old when he suddenly became very ill. He was a healthy baby, so it wasn't easy to see that he was sick. I knew something was horribly wrong when his bowel movement became runny and every fifteen minutes. Polad and I took him to the ER and there the doctor started arguing with us that this baby didn't look that sick! He was grabbing baby's chubby stomach telling us:
"See; he hasn't lost a lot of fluid. It is all in your mind."

I was about to scream at the doctor, but Polad pulled him aside and told him something. Suddenly, they admitted Amir into the hospital! They told us that he had some sort of a violent virus in his system, so he was given an IV through the vein on his ankle. As soon as he was a little hydrated he got up and pulled the needle out of his vein! They fixed the situation and wanted to tie his little arms, but I begged them not to do that. So, instead they put a lot of tapes on the needle. It was a horrible experience to see my baby on the hospital bed. Finally, after three nights, the doctor prescribed some medical drops that were an extract from opium.

###

When my dad was with us in Iran, things were better for me and Amir. Polad would leave the house in the morning to work at his organization, and Amir and I would be alone unless my dad was home with us. My dad didn't have a car anymore and Polad would use my car as if it was his! That was very irritating for my father who had paid for that car for me! He used to say:

"Your husband is really selfish; what if we need to take Amir to a doctor or something? How can he just take the car with no shame?"

I knew Polad HAD to have a car. In his line of activities the last thing he needed was to be alongside the road waiting for a cab or bus! Amir was about one year old when we realized that I was expecting again.

###

One day, as my father was away, Polad and I had some of his friends over to the house. I was in the kitchen frying onions which is often the first step of making any Persian food! The "boys" had gathered in the hallway on the first floor and were doing target practice, aiming with a practice hand gun. This black, heavy hand-gun looked very real, but it only took pellets. I could hear them talking and laughing. Polad called me and asked:

"Can you come here for a minute?" I left my cooking, walked out of the kitchen and said:

"What do you need?" He had a little smile on his face and handed me the gun and said:

"That is the target. Will you shoot a few for us?"

"Sure," I said, and as I took the gun from him he turned to his friends and said:

"Watch this!" I aimed and shot right in the center of the target across the hallway, handed him the gun and said:

"Anything else?" They all began laughing and cheering for me; he seemed to be very proud of his little wife and I loved it!

Amir was not yet two and one of his games was to run around our old formal living room. He ran into one of our heavy dining-room chairs and blood was soon gushing out of his mouth. It was around 6 p.m. and I didn't have the car, and I was four months pregnant! My dad grabbed Amir and we rushed out towards the closest hospital which was about half a mile away. My father was breathing hard and I had been in such a hurry to leave the house that I had put on my dad's flip flops, which were far too big for me! As we arrived at the ER, we were told that the ER was closed because there had been an intake of so many war wounded soldiers.

We started walking again, this time towards a small medical center that was about another half a mile away. When we arrived there the doctor looked at Amir's mouth and told us that we needed to find a hospital that would have surgical equipment for children! I pleaded with him to do something, but he replied that as he didn't have the special needle to do the stitches, his work would have left Amir's lip bumpy and ugly. I was devastated – my son was crying and spitting blood. Dad and I didn't have a car to go to the Children's Hospital, and we were thinking about hitting the road again, walking to the main street and waiting for a taxi.

As we were debating upon that, I heard some noise from the waiting room. Someone had just walked in and was talking to the staff in a friendly way. We walked out of the doctor's office into the waiting room and I saw a young doctor in his white uniform. He looked at us and asked what had happened. We told him and he said:

"Wait a minute. I think I have one of those small needles in my pocket!"

He was a small children's surgery specialist and he had just walked in to say hello to his old friends. I know how unbelievable this story may sound, but it happened just as I described. The angels were with us! He fixed the inner upper lip of Amir's mouth and we walked back home. Amir is a 30 year old fine looking young man now and there is no sign of that injury on his lip. This is an example of one instance when the Universe was working with me.

When we were living at my dad's house Polad was busy with his activities without thinking that where we were living was not HIS house. All kinds of people would come and go, or even stay there. My dad, who had moved downstairs to the old living room didn't say anything to us, but I knew he wasn't happy with his home turning into some sort of a safe-house for an underground political organization.

One day, when I was alone with baby Amir, after putting him down for a nap, I sat on the stairs of the porch. Remember that I grew up in that house and I had always sat there to think and look at the birds, sky and other people's windows… That early evening, I sat on the steps and thought to myself: let's find the "happy homes". I always did that as a kid. I would look at the neighbors' windows, and based on the movements of the curtains, or the lighting, or the sound of people coming out, or the flower pots on the edges, I would decide if they were happy or sad homes! Here I was twenty years later doing the same thing. I looked at the second floor window of the house across the alley from ours. I could see the white sheer curtain moving with the wind. I knew they were a young couple who had just married a few months ago. I could hear them talking and cooking together. I decided that it was a happy home and felt very jealous that I was so lonely in my life.

A week after that, Polad came home one night and told me that his friends were coming over for dinner. That night we had six or seven very important people from his organization in our house. I don't know the occasion for that gathering, but it must have been a very important one. They were all happy and talking together; the sound of laughter was taking over that large house like in the old days. I don't know why, but someone said that our street had felt a bit different when he was coming over…

I volunteered to grab the baby Amir and walk towards the intersection as if I was going to buy some yogurt. I put on my old wool cape, covered my hair with a scarf, held Amir in my arms and walked out. I walked straight and fast towards the intersection where there were two stores, I knew very well that they were both closed at 9 p.m. but I acted as if I didn't know. As I walked out of our alley I saw a white sedan with three or four big shadows in it, which was parked across the street from our alley. I could see the shadows moving and the small lights of the car were on so the engine was running.

I had seen what I was there to see, but passed them and walked towards the intersection. I arrived at the store's door, looked up, touched the door knob and turned around towards the house, all to keep up the pretense. Back home, I informed Polad about the white car and the people inside, so our guests became quiet and nobody left our house that night. A few weeks later, I found out that that very night they had captured the young couple from across the alley, in the middle of the night and taken them away. I felt so ashamed of myself for being jealous of them the other day. They never came back and the landlord gave their stuff to their family later on so that he could rent out the second floor to new tenants.

Moving again – July 1983

When I was about seven months pregnant with our second child, Polad found a little apartment for us and we moved out of my father's house. It took me a while to call this apartment "home". As much as I always wanted to get out of that house and have my own place, living there as an adult was giving me a very secure feeling. Childhood homes are a part of our being that almost seems to be embedded in our soul. All of those corners that you grew up discovering, one by one.

Nobody else knew about the color of the wall behind that closet door or the place on the basement wall where you wrote your name, when you were 6 years old. All of those little places that you used to hide in and nobody could find you. The only place in the world that you could run to and be safe forever was your home.

Home, where Mom and Dad protected you, where you ruled and nobody was allowed to hurt you. We all come to the point of leaving "home" in our lives, sooner or later. The time comes that we need to move on and create our own sanctuary for the generation for which we will become the protectors. So we left the large house to go to this little apartment. I was alone with the baby all the time, and Polad was busy with his fight against the bad guys, to save Iran and eventually the whole world.

I remember, in one of our discussions, he said that the society structure in Iran was wrong. I can't quote his words exactly, but the gist of what he said was that the big gap between the classes in society was wrong, and the whole world needed to stand up to that problem. He was right, I could clearly see the difference between how I grew up and how the majority of people in Iran had lived for many generations, I just wasn't sure if his way was the right one. He wanted to keep me out of his activities for my own sake, and his friends probably thought I was too stupid to understand their cause to join them.

As far as I was concerned, there wasn't much anybody could do for the large population of illiterate and mentally held back people, who simply weren't educated enough to understand what was best for them. I know that I sound pretty snobbish saying this, but how did they expect to convince the people who still believed that seeing a woman's hair would allow them to rape her and that wouldn't be their fault; how did they expect these people to understand anything regarding economy, education and most importantly, equal rights for the sexes?

Ah, my mistake; they thought that they would have to "make" them follow. Okay, so they were talking about a "dictatorship" over the plebeians again, weren't they? Well, that was the part that I didn't agree with. I was called an ideologist and a dreamer for that, but I truly have never seen any difference between any party from another which would dictate to the population, when each party was all about "controlling" people.

For me, the only way to save the human race is education and education only. What I'm talking about is a true opportunity for all people to learn everything so that they can decide for themselves, so that they will take action in an appropriate way. An illustration is in order. In one of the movements people got into an army ammunitions store and many weapons were released to no matter whom. I would be driving along and, to my frightened dismay, discover someone directing traffic at an intersection with a machine gun. They would be shooting and ordering people to go in this or that direction. I liken it to giving a huge knife to a three year old! It was not only frightening, but pathetic… That's why I say education is the answer. It doesn't matter if you have a tank or a machine gun. If people's brains aren't engaged in the right way – knowing what is right or wrong – no one will get anywhere.

Isn't development the object of all life? Everyone living on this planet, no matter where they are, has the right to attain as much development as they can or as they wish for. Surely, everyone naturally wants to become the best they can be. Education aids them in that quest. No one can live fully or advance without an education.

The Shah's Secret Police "SAVAK" tortured Iranians for decades for owning a book that was written by Carl Marx or anybody with the same line of thoughts. True education allows people to learn about all the different views, to then be able to reach the decision that is best for them. But hey, who was I to say anything to all of these hot blooded young people who never held a second thought about bleeding to death for Iran?

Well, I will share my thoughts in more depth here so that you understand where I am coming from on this subject, what my vision is of the real Iran, and what I'd like to see emerging in Iran – people being who they are and living together…

When I was going to school, there was a Jewish kid with the Star of David necklace round her neck, a Muslim girl who always wore a little scarf on her head, and a Christian kid wearing a cross. We all played together and no one put anyone else down. We all watched and talked about the same television shows. We were all running around the same schoolyard. That is the real Iran for me – the focus being lifted from what your religious beliefs are and put on what your society can do to develop. That's what I'd like to see. Maybe I am a dreamer. Perhaps in a country with that many illiterate people it's not easy to come to that state, but those are my childhood memories showing that people from different religious backgrounds can get on and live together, in a fully functioning manner.

Of course, before the revolution, the Shah was in power and what he was presenting and providing was for the minority of the population. I've been told and have read about a lot of cities and villages where people were living in bad conditions, a far cry from the conditions in which I grew up. I'm not being blind to that. I realize this. But, when I spoke to these socialists in the seventies they would tell me that for a rich, but illiterate country like Iran, there's no happy ending in the near future. They said that Iran would need a constructive dictatorship to push the people and society towards the right path. I refuse to believe that…

I believe there's still hope to have people understanding and educated. Start by pumping the religion out of people a bit. Too much religion leads to people being under-developed and stops them from trying to find out more, to have more knowledge, to read more, grasp more – because they feel comfy in their own little "cave" of religious narrow-mindedness – to put it bluntly. I'm not insulting anyone religious. I want to make that clear. But what I witnessed in Iran, with the new Islamic regime, was people being kept backward with religious oppression.

Some religious people refuse to see the world growing and to accept anything new. They are judgmental without even knowing about these new things, because they are blinded by their religious leaders and the beliefs and paradigms they follow within their religion – very often due to fear. What god would really want their creations acting out of fear? God/Source wouldn't want blinkered creations milling about blindly. God/Source would want their creations being lovingly creative and following in their footsteps… enjoying the world in which they have been created.

Finally, my heart warmed up towards that little place, and I fell in love with my little one bedroom apartment that I could clean in less than twenty minutes! We put Amir's old bed in the room that was the entrance to the apartment, for the new baby, and a normal bed on the other side of the same room for Amir.

Amir playing with some friends in his little corner of the apartment.

I was in my last month of pregnancy when one evening we decided to pay a visit to one of Polad's friends. Their house was quite a distance from ours. As Polad was driving he mentioned that we should stay there for the night. I really didn't feel like sleeping anywhere else but my own bed. The last few weeks of pregnancy are hard enough and nobody likes to sleep on the floor! We had a fight in the car and I threatened to get out of the car with Amir and take a cab back home! Polad turned the car around and drove back home…

One hour later, as I was quietly cleaning the place, and ironing Polad's shirts, the baby started knocking! I had taken 23 month old Amir to the bathroom when I saw the puddle of water on the floor. I thought Amir had had an accident, so I tried to bend over to clean the floor, when I felt the push! I realized that my waters had broken, and I don't know why, but I was so calm and continued ironing his shirts! Then I emptied his large ashtray and told him:

"It's time; take Amir -- we need to go now! He carried sleeping Amir and I grabbed my pre-packed bag and we quietly took the stairs of four stories down to get in the car.

The hospital that I was supposed to go to was only fifteen minutes from our place, and it was a miracle that we hadn't gone to the other side of Tehran that night, to visit his friends. The pressure was unbelievable, and as soon as I lay down on the hospital bed, my baby girl Maral was born at 9 p.m. on October 10th of 1983 with no problem. My little girl was very small, with big dark eyes and a very light skin. She was beautiful.

When I came home with the new baby, Polad took Amir to work with him to give me a day or two to recover and pull myself together. Little Amir was so cute and smart, but instead of starting to talk he liked to mimic talking! He would do a complete facial impression and move his little arms up and down (as we Iranians do while talking), and say total gibberish as if he was making a very important speech. It was so cute seeing him doing that. I used to look at him very seriously, as if I knew what he was talking about, and nod my head and say things to him like:

"Sure, I agree with you; we will definitely do it that way"!

When baby Maral was born, Amir was still young enough to take a bottle every now and then. I will never forget the day that I put them both on the bed with their bottles, and Amir was holding his bottle with one hand and the baby's bottle with the other! I wish I had taken a picture of them.

Going from that joyous note, I will now get to the point of the ultimate challenge…

Chapter Ten

Free Falling on the Rocks (Numb Revisited)

8:00 p.m., October 25th, 1983

Maral was 15 days old and Amir's second birthday was approaching. That night Polad came home with a package that he had received from his brother in the US. He was happy, but his face was so tired and full of anxiety. He told me that he wanted to open it with me. Upon opening the package we discovered two very pretty snow suits for the kids and that made our day. Polad held baby Maral in his arms and did a few slow dance moves with her; then he said:
"Tell her that the first man she danced with was her father." I made a face and said:
"Stop it, you will tell her yourself."

That night he told me to pack a suitcase because we had to leave the apartment for a while. I looked at his face; he looked stressed out and I could see the dark circles under his eyes. He wasn't feeling well in those days. He had the serious stomach problem –the bleeding ulcer. He was only 29 years old, but I knew that he was under a lot of stress due to his political activities.

I replied that I wouldn't pack, and he could pack and go wherever he wanted. He told me that it was not about choice and I HAD to leave the apartment with him that night. I understood that it was not a normal situation, so I packed one medium size suitcase for me and the kids and one small bag for Polad. I was mad at him for forcing his opinion on me once again so I wasn't talking to him, and held a cold attitude all the way to his friend's house.

Both babies were asleep when we arrived at Nader and Susan's little place. Susan's mother was there too. As always we were greeted with smiles and help with the babies. The place was too hot for me, but I really couldn't say anything because we were making their small place become even smaller. There were too many people in one room. The room actually consisted of two spaces, as if there used to be a door in the middle, way back in time. Maral began crying. She was a very weak child who wouldn't drink milk very comfortably. She was a true cry baby! Everybody was kind and loving and held her for a few minutes. Nader said:

"Wow, this one has a big voice like her brother too!"

Little Amir had somehow caused a little boo-boo on his chubby little finger and was about to make a lot of fuss when "Uncle Nader" produced a little construction tape with some cotton in the middle of it, telling him that it was a special Band-Aid, just for good boys like Amir! That night, we slept in those "two" rooms with a drape hanging in the middle. The men slept on one side of the curtain, the women and children on the other.

I can't remember if Polad left Nader's place sometime after we went to bed that night or the next morning. I didn't see him leave and wasn't talking to him anyway…

It was the day after and I was expecting Polad to come back to get us at any minute. It was 6 p.m. and I was listening to the noises from the road through the window that was above my eye level. Time turned and turned. It was 8 p.m. and Susan said that we should eat something. I put the babies in bed in the corner of the room and sat there waiting and waiting. Polad would never stay out that late; he was normally home before 8 p.m. Time was moving on and there was no sign of my husband. Nader was in and out of the room. It seemed as if he and Susan were avoiding any eye contact with me. Susan's mother, who was a small lively woman was talking, laughing and helping her daughter with their little baby girl "Shady".

I was waiting…and the time turned to midnight. I had a feeling that something horrible had happened, but didn't want to believe it. That little place was too hot for November and I was feeling nauseous. Maral woke up and I tried to breast feed her, but she refused and turned her face away. She was crying, but didn't want to drink the milk… I changed her diaper and she wouldn't calm down. I picked her up and began marching back and forth in that little space, moving her up and down and whispering in her ears that she had to go to sleep. I was so concerned that Amir would wake up and ask for his father… Finally, Maral went back to sleep and I put her down just as Nader came into the room, looking so pale that there was no mistaking that he had some very bad news.

He got close to me and whispered: "I think they got him." I looked at the clock and it was 2:30 a.m. I had known in my heart that he wouldn't come back that night, but hearing it from Nader made it as real and lonely as I had ever felt in my life. I was staring at Nader's mouth, hoping that there would be something more that he hadn't told me yet. Something around the lines of "….but we know where he is," or "we know someone who can give us more information about his situation," but there was nothing else left for him to say. I did not cry… I was just standing there thinking about my children…

It was about 6 a.m. and Nader and I were standing very close to each other whispering, when Susan's mother rushed into the room and back out again, screaming at her daughter. I could hear her saying: "YOU ARE BLIND. YOU DON'T WANT TO SEE WHAT IS RIGHT BEFORE YOUR EYES."

Susan rushed into the room and, with panic resonating in her voice, told me and her husband to stay away from each other because her mother was under the impression that we were having an affair! The problem was that years ago she had been cheated on by her husband and now, as nobody could tell her what was happening for security reasons, she couldn't digest the picture of her son-in-law being so secretive with another woman.

The Journey Begins

By 10 or 11 a.m. Nader approached me and requested that I leave their house, and I perfectly understood his reasons. He had to protect his family and there was no reason for me to stay there and bring the government's secret service to that house. He said:
"You need to go to a family member's house and not a friend's place."
I said that I had no family left in Iran; they were all in the US. He asked me to think hard and I did, but still couldn't come up with anybody. I knew that my father's brother was still living in Tehran and when we were children we used to play a lot with our cousins, but I hadn't had any contact with them for over ten years.

Finally, I told him that I knew a family in Tehran's suburbs that was related to my brother-in-law's wife, and they were the only "family" that I could bring to mind. One problem was that Polad had left with my car. Besides, I didn't really know how to get to that family's house either. The other problem was that they belonged to the minority religion like my mother's family and I wasn't even sure if they would feel safe taking us in. One of Polad's buddies, Sepehr was friends with one of the daughters in that family, so he was volunteered to take me and the babies there.

He arrived at Nader's place to take us. Nader gave me 5000 Rilas (IRR) (about $60 US back then). I didn't want to take the money because I knew he didn't have any money to spare, but I realized that I had to take it. I had no money and couldn't go back home to grab my bank booklet. I had some money left in my savings account from the time that my parents used to give me some money, even after I got married.

He helped me with the suitcase and the babies; we took a cab to the bus station on the other side of Tehran. We sat in the bus as if we were a normal little family. He was holding one baby on his knee and I had the other one in my arms. We didn't talk much. I was still numb, and he was probably thinking about what would happen if they stopped us and asked questions. He didn't know anything about me to pretend that we were related in any shape or form.

During the bus trip, as I was looking outside, through the window, I remembered when my dad used to take us to the shore house every year. He would be driving; Mom would be holding my baby sister on her knee, singing and my brother and I would fight on the back seat! I became enraged by remembering the past. I became angry with Polad. How dare he gamble our lives like that? What did he think would happen to me and our children if he was captured? I had a college degree, but he never let me get a job. Besides, how would I go to work with two children under two years old?

I was getting angrier by the minute. I remembered one conversation with Polad, when Amir was only one year old, and that put fire in my heart. We were in the car. Polad was driving and we passed a large dumpster area with little dirty children playing around it. I told Polad to back off from his activities a bit, and I said:
"What if you and I both get captured? What will happen to Amir? You don't want him to become homeless and grow up around city dumpsters do you?" His answer was:
"Many children in this world grow up around city dumpsters, so what if one of them is my child?"

He must have counted on my father taking care of us. But he knew that my father had his own life with the other woman and was traveling between the US and Iran. I felt so angry and so powerful to prove it to him that I was not the "cotton wrapped princess", as he used to call me. The resilient middle child woke up in me. I was a survivor and it was time to stand up and do what I was best at, SURVIVING! All of those years I hadn't known that it was anger that made me so strong. It has just become known to me, as I'm writing this memoir, that I became so furious at him that I had to show him what I was made of.

How could he gamble like that and lose us? I understood the meaning of self-sacrificing for a valuable goal. I understood the meaning of war and the possibility of not coming back, but I had never heard of sacrificing someone else for your goals. Knowing his goal in life, he had had no right to get married, and when he did, he had no business bringing children into this world. It feels so bad saying this, because it seems as if I'm wishing that my two children had never been born, but why didn't he think about us when he was trying to save humanity? He knew where he was headed, so why hadn't he set me up with a job first? Why had he never let me to go to work? What did he think would happen when he was gone? Why was he so sure that my father would step in and take over HIS financial and emotional responsibilities?

The bus arrived and we grabbed the children and began walking towards their house. As soon as we saw the house down the street Sepehr asked me if I knew where I was. When I told him that I did, he said that he would go back to Tehran, but if at any time I needed anything I should let him know...

I rang the doorbell and my sister-in-law's mother, Miss Rose opened the door. She was happy and stretched her arms out to grab one of the babies from me. She was a very kind woman and always said that my children reminded her of her own grandchildren whom she hadn't seen for years. Her daughter and son-in-law had moved to the US a while back. As she was helping me inside said:

"Welcome dear, welcome. Where is Polad?"

As soon as she saw the suitcase she knew! We went inside without the suitcase and her husband welcomed us too. He asked about Polad, and I said:

"He is parking the car; he'll be in, in a few minutes."

Miss Rose started preparing lunch and I got busy attending to the children. Miss Rose's husband said:

"Why are you serving the lunch without waiting for Polad?"

Miss Rose said: "Well, it may take a few years for him to park the car!"

Miss Rose's husband, Mr. Shaker span round to face me giving me a horrified look as if he was saying: Is this true? And what the hell are you doing here?

I immediately looked away, pretending that I hadn't seen his look. Miss Rose changed the subject to the lunch and the children to give me a few minutes to pull myself together.

Miss Rose and her husband had three daughters. One was my sister-in-law and the other two were still living at home. By the evening, the girls had come home from work and discovered my situation. The younger one, who was friends with Sepehr, showed sympathy, but the older daughter wasn't happy with me and my children for being there. I couldn't blame her, knowing how worried she must have been for her elderly parents.

By the evening, they put a large mattress on their living room floor for me and the kids to spend the night. During the night Mr. Shaker, who was obviously very worried about us being there, was constantly walking from their bedroom to the kitchen and back. Each time, he had to watch his step so as not to step on us on the floor!

Maral wouldn't sleep or drink milk. She was fussing all night. I used to have lots of milk when I had Amir, but nothing for this poor baby. Eventually, I tried to feed her with baby formula by bottle, but she was not a happy camper. Miss Rose's youngest daughter, Sepeedeh was very kind and sweet with me and the children. She would stay up during the night to take turns in holding and walking the crying baby and talk to me.

During our stay at their house Amir's birthday arrived. He was turning two, so they kindly bought a cake and we celebrated his birthday and took a few pictures.

The first morning, Mr. Shaker told me that we should go to Polad's half-cousin's house to see if he could help us with the situation. I truly don't remember how we got there. I mean, I'm sure I didn't know the address and Mr. Shaker wouldn't know it either, but somehow he drove me and the kids to that house. I had met Polad's half-cousin, Farhad and his family maybe twice before, so I wasn't really feeling comfortable going there, but what could I say to Mr. Shaker? When we arrived Farhad, who had just arrived from work, was pulling into his driveway.

We went in and sat down. I kept myself busy with Maral and Amir and let Mr. Shaker handle the visit. I remember that I felt so hot in their house and my ears felt as if they were on fire. I was very embarrassed and didn't know what to say or do. Finally, I looked up and my eyes met Farhad's. He was looking at me with great sorrow, but somehow made it clear to Mr. Shaker that I couldn't stay in their house due to his own previous underground activities. Mr. Shaker was not happy at all. We thanked them for the tea and drove back to Mr. Shaker's house. Later on Farhad told me that he had had to really control himself to not slap Mr. Shaker who had taken us to his house, like some stray animals that he needed to get rid of.

Time to Leave

Amir was changing. He was not that co-operative a little toddler any more. I could see that he was becoming a rebellious child. I was trying to have some "one on one" time with him. Any time that I could put Maral down for a nap I would sit with Amir and talk to him and tell him how much I loved him. I would tell him stories and act out the different characters with different voices, to see the sparkle in his beautiful big black eyes.

Amir's lonely second Birthday while we were at Miss Rose's house

I think it was the third day of our stay there that I thought I should find a way to pay them some money to help with the food and generally show my appreciation. All the money that I had was the $60.00 that Nader had given me. Miss Rose had some items on her dining room table for the neighbors to buy. Among those items, there were some baby clothes and a blanket that had belonged to my sister-in-law's baby girl. So I offered to purchase those and they accepted. I was very happy to do that and I knew I could get money later on, from selling some items that we had in my childhood house.

I think it was the fifth day that we had been there when the older daughter came home from work, and as she walked in she said:
"Ah, you guys are *still* here?"

That night I wrote a very small note saying: "Our landlord needs the room and we need to move. Please help!" I folded the note very small and asked Sepeedeh to take it to Sepehr the next day. She used to go to Tehran for work every day so she took the note to deliver it for me. The next night when she came home she had a note for me that said: "We'll pick you and the kids up on Thursday between 2 and 4 p.m." I had no idea where I was going to be taken or who "we" were!

Only a few days after Polad's disappearance when I arrived at Miss Rose's house with two suit cases and two babies. Here I am holding new born Maral as sweet "Sepeedeh" is holding sad, grumpy Amir who is looking for his dad every hour of every day.

On Wednesday night I told Miss Rose's family that I was leaving the next day and greatly thanked them for their hospitality. Their youngest daughter, stayed up most of the night with me and we talked about my children. She was telling me that everything would be just fine. She was about four or five years younger than me, and didn't have any children, so it was somewhat difficult for me to believe in what she was telling me! Actually, I don't believe I was even thinking about the future at that point. All I was thinking about was the next day and perhaps the day after that. I was thinking about my apartment and all of my belongings in there. I was thinking about my dad's house with all the furnished rooms, and here I was, moving from and into people's houses like a beggar.

The next day arrived; the young girl couldn't stop crying. Poor thing was shaking and crying, knowing that it was possibly the last time she'd see me and my children again. Miss Rose was trying to calm her down, joking that nobody cries when house guests are leaving, but someone like Sepeedeh!

We were standing outside the door, in the alley waiting when Sepehr walked into the alley towards the house. He smiled and took the suitcase from me. I kissed Miss Rose and Sepeedeh took Amir's hand and followed him away from the house, carrying my baby girl in the other arm. Immediately at the end of the alley there was a little yellow car and I recognized one of Polad's friend's wives who was in the driver's seat. We got in, said hello and were soon driving towards Tehran. Sepehr was interacting with Amir in the car to keep him occupied. He told me that we were going to his house for a while! I nodded my head and thanked him.

Chapter Eleven

Fun Life
Ten Days after Polad was Captured

I had never met Sepehr's wife and children before, so when we arrived I was trying to be as quiet and invisible as possible, but walking in with a 2 year old child and a month old crying baby just wasn't being quiet and invisible! His wife, Parvin was a beautiful slender young woman with long straight black hair. She seemed to be very reserved, so we had no encounters for the first day or two. Sepehr, on the other hand, was so lively and knew how to deal with Amir. He brought a lot of large papers and coloring pencils and told Amir to draw whatever he wanted. Magic happened; Amir began to draw lines in different colors and talking with him as if he had known him all his life.

My little boy had missed his father so bad that he was bonding with this stranger in a heart-beat. Sepehr was a very nice person and they had two young children themselves, so Amir had children around to play with too. After a few days his wife and I connected also. It was fun to be with that family. The children would play all day, Parvin and I would clean the house and cook together and at night, friends would show up for a bite to eat, drinking some homemade vodka and listening to good music.

It was 1983 and Iran had had no updated music or movies since the revolution that had happed in 1979. Sepehr had his connections with the outside world, so he had music videos and some movies too. In their house we saw Michael Jackson's "Thriller", Cyndi Lauper's "Girls Just Want to Have Fun" and Pink Floyd's "Wall Part 2" for the first time! Amir started to relax; he loved music and he loved drawing. With him improving I started feeling more comfortable too and even started to breast feed baby Maral again!

Parvin and Sepehr were very nice people and they made us feel very comfortable and happy. I told them that Polad didn't get a chance to get a birth certificate for Maral and I needed that to get food coupons from the local "Committee". Fortunately, I had grabbed the hospital birth certificate when we left the apartment, so Sepehr took that document and went to the related office and obtained the legal Birth Certificate for Maral. I still don't know how he did it. He must have introduced himself as Polad!

After a week or so of being there I realized that it was time for me to do something other than hiding in other people's houses. That life couldn't be continued forever and I needed to start a normal daily life and routine for the children. The fact that Polad was not captured from our apartment was a good sign that I could probably go back there, but it was still a risky situation. My childhood house, on the other hand, seemed to be the perfect place, but I needed to check it out first to see if the neighbors had seen anything or anybody that could have been alarming. The other important matter was that there was a telephone line in my dad's house, but I had no telephone in our apartment.

One afternoon I asked Parvin to keep an eye on the children for a few hours, so I could go to my old neighborhood and check out the house. I thought I knew exactly where Sepehr and Parvin's house was, but since I didn't pay any attention while they were taking us there coming back to it could have been a problem. Also, for some reason my eyesight had become extremely bad within the last two weeks since Polad had disappeared on us. Maybe it had been getting bad during the past few years after having two babies and I had never had a reason to notice it. Or perhaps I was experiencing a psychological reaction – not letting myself see or hear what was going on, retaining that numbness as a cocoon to protect myself...

Sepehr told me that I had two hours to come back. He said if I wasn't back within two hours he would consider me as captured and he would destroy all of his information. He also said that if I wasn't back by that night he would move everybody out of his house, I agreed and left their house, covering myself in a black "chador" so people wouldn't recognize me.

Pretender

I ought to remind you that I had never worn a chador before and I didn't own one, so I borrowed one from Parvin and took a crash course about how to hold it under my chin by one hand and walk as if everything was just normal! I tell you, it wasn't easy at all. It kept sliding off my head and I had to make sure not to show the hair on top. It was opening in front like a curtain on a windy day and I had to secure it with the other hand from inside...

I took a cab and arrived in my old neighborhood. The good thing about that area was that most of the people were from different religious minorities. All the houses across the alley from our house were owned by Zoroastrians who were extremely private and peaceful people. The rest of the people were Armenians or Muslims who had probably never seen inside a Mosque in their lives!

I walked into our alley and knocked at the neighbor's house that was straight across from ours. She opened the window and didn't recognize me at first. After I showed her my full face she started laughing and said:
"I wonder what your mom would say if she could see you wearing that thing!"

I talked to her and she assured me that nobody was watching the house and nobody came to ask questions about me or Polad. It was wonderful news! As I was thanking her and getting ready to leave she said: "Azita, you look a little awkward in that chador." I asked her to explain what she meant, and she said that it showed that I didn't know how to handle it, so I should be careful.

I walked back to the main street and took a cab to the nearest circle to my host's house to walk the rest of the way. On my way I bought a big paper bag of tangerines and started walking. The sidewalk was so crowded; people were walking fast and women were holding their chador while carrying babies as if it was nothing! I walked up and then I walked down the street without being able to find the back road to their house. I knew that my uncle's three story house was nearby. I walked towards their house and found it. After I knocked at the door one of my cousins looked out of the upper level windows, I said "Hello" and asked if anybody was home. I wasn't about to tell her any details of my situation, but I was hoping if I could get inside I could use the phone book and find Sepehr's home phone number.

Unfortunately, thanks to a lot of family disputes between us and them, she was not interested in letting me in. I'm sure if she had known what was going on, I would have been inside in a flash, but I didn't want to involve them in any possible problem that I was in. So, I walked back to the main street, trying to find Sepehr's narrow alley. It was getting late and every time I heard a baby crying my breasts would get a rush of milk which was becoming very painful. Dusk was beginning to fall, and I was so scared about being away from my children. I saw a woman with two children walking towards me; without exchanging one word, I handed her the four pound bag of tangerines and walked away.

I went up and down the street maybe four times and suddenly a "Pasdar" (Islamic soldier from the local committee) stopped me and said:
"Sister, do you live around here?"

I looked towards him and without staring in his face said:
"Well no brother!"
"I have been watching you for a while, going up and down the street. Are you looking for something or *someone*?" he said.

It dawned on me that he thought I was a prostitute looking for customers, so to avoid any further disasters I tried to talk like someone who wasn't from Tehran and replied:

"Brother, I'm not from here, I'm visiting some friends and I can't find their house."

I told him that my brother-in-law had put me and my children on the bus from Arak (a small town near Tehran), and the friends picked us up from the bus station and took us to their house. Then I had left to get diapers and milk for the babies and had got lost on my way back there.

He suggested taking me to the local committee so we could find my host's house address and phone number through the list of people who were getting food coupons. I agreed, knowing that it was not right to take any of those people to Sepehr's house, but I was desperate and needed to get back to my children as soon as possible. He showed the way and I followed. When we arrived at the committee and went in he said:

"Ah, I forgot that the chief is not here right now. As you know, it is time for the evening prayers and he must be in the mosque. Why don't you go to the mosque across the street and do your evening prayers and come back in one hour? Allah will hear you, since tonight is our innocent murdered Imam Hussein's anniversary."

"Yes, of course, brother. I will do that and will be back here in one hour. May Allah bless you and your family," I said and walked towards the mosque.

As I was walking there I thought: Just perfect; I should have learned the Islamic prayers in school. They had an Islamic Religious Class for everybody twice a week starting at second grade. It was no time to think like that; I had to go through whatever was coming my way to get to be with Amir and Maral again. I had never been in a mosque before. I had visited one or two during my life when sightseeing the historical buildings. I walked into the big yard and saw a group of women wearing the black chador, who were gathered around something, I walked directly towards them. As I got closer I realized that I had made the right decision. They were around the water valves doing the special ablutions before praying.

With apologies to all of my Muslim friends and families, I find this a ridiculous Islamic rule. You see, this "wash up" doesn't actually clean anything. You have to wet your index finger, say some Arabic words from the Quran and draw a line from the tip of your big toe to the high bone of your foot. You do the same on your other foot; then you take a fistful of water and throw it on your elbow while holding your arm pointing downwards to the ground. Then you come to your face; you wet your index finger and draw a line from the forehead to the middle of your head. All done. You are clean to start your prayers…

Here I was, next to the she crows (as my sister and I used to call women in the black chador), and I started doing the same ritual and whispering to myself, as if I was saying the words of the Quran; then I followed some of them into the mosque. It was a large and very bright room smelling like a mixture of body odor and food. I instantly gagged, but held my head down and looked around out of the corners of my eyes. There was a huge curtain in the middle of the room that went from the ceiling to the floor. I could see shapes and shadows of men walking or praying on the other side of the curtain.

The corner of the curtain came up and a man's arm was revealed, holding a tray of "Sholeh Zard" (Iranian rice pudding with Saffron and Cinnamon). A woman reached out, grabbed the tray and held it out in front of the others. The man's arm appeared again holding another tray; this time it was "Halva" (a pastry that they make with oil, flour, sugar and rose water). I grabbed that tray and followed the other woman, holding it out in front of the others!

Then I realized that whether I liked it or not I HAD to start the prayers, so I stood next to an old woman who was in the middle of her prayers. She went down on her knees putting her palms on the floor and her forehead in between her hands; I went down and did exactly the same. I was looking at her from the corner of my eye to see when she got up, so I could follow! She moved, so I started getting up. Damn, she didn't get up, so I went back down thinking "The old bitch is testing me!" She got up and put her hands on the side of her head with her palms open. I did the same, remembering my brother and I used to make faces at each other just like that. I kept my chuckle to myself and tried to keep a straight face, moving my lips as if I was praying…

Oh my God, it seemed as if she was going down again… No, she stopped half way, bending over with her hands on her knees, and I followed. She sat down and started saying "Allah O Akbar" (God is great) many times, so I did the same. She turned to me and said:
"Sister, why did you do "broken" prayers? I instantly realized that when I arrived she had already done some of her prayers, so I only finished one set. But the evening prayers are two sets, so I said:
"Sister, I did the first set at home and the other one here by your side."
I have no idea if such a thing is possible and didn't pay any attention to her suspicious looks as I walked out!

I was sweating, and under the chador, the front of my shirt was wet from the milk rush. I walked back to the Committee building and the door was closed. I dropped down on the steps and wept…I didn't know what to do any more. Suddenly, I heard footsteps, raised my head and saw the same Pasdar who had guided me there walking towards me. I pulled the chador closer around my face and looked up. He said;
"Sister isn't the chief here?"
"No," I said, "and I really need to talk with him."
"He must have gone home after the prayers; he lives around the corner -- let me walk you there. I felt uncomfortable doing so, but I had no other choice. I agreed and followed him, still in tears. I was truly crying and didn't see any reason for hiding it.

He knocked at a door and a man in his fifties opened it. The Pasdar and he welcomed each other and the chief soon found out that I was a stranger in Tehran, who was visiting friends and got lost. He offered to walk back to the committee to help me, by looking at names and addresses. I followed them back to the committee building, and he asked for the resident's full name. With the same pretend accent, I told him that I only knew the first name -- Sepehr. He said that there were many guys living in that area with that name, and he really needed the last name. When I told him that I couldn't remember it, he offered for me to spend the night at his house, and he would come back to the committee with me in the morning to find the "Sepehr" that I was talking about. The Pasdar intervened and suggested that I could stay at his house… Great; now they were fighting over who would get to rape me that night!

I suddenly hit myself in the chest, opened my arms, then tilted my head back to face towards the ceiling and said:
"Imam Hussein, help me to remember, Imam Hussein help me, help me…" and put my head between my hands and started swaying my body back and forth and sideways.
"THIS WORTHLESS PEASANT OF YOUR RIGHTEOUSNESS IS THANKFUL MY IMAM," I shouted and turned to the two men shrieking:
"I REMEMBERED!"

The chief found Sepehr's file and began dialing their phone number. I continued my "sudden joy" and kept talking out loud to "Imam Hussein" and circling the chief on the phone. I was very loud and thanking Imam Hussein for helping me to remember the last name of my host. On the other end of the telephone line, Sepehr heard me and realized that I was okay, he told me later. The chief started his conversation on the phone with:
"Hey brother, aren't you worried for this woman who left your house, to buy diapers and milk for her babies, a while ago and hasn't come back yet?"
Sepehr told me that he had immediately responded with:
"Yes brother we are; we have been calling all the hospitals to see if she was hit by a car or something. Thank you, thank you very much for calling us!"

The chief told Sepehr that he would walk me to their house and he did so. As soon as Sepehr hung up the phone he told his wife that the Committee's Chief was on his way to their house with me, and she should get rid of the vodka immediately.

When we arrived, Parvin was standing in front of the house wearing a chador, holding screaming Maral in her arms and Amir was standing with Sepehr. Parvin's face had a weird smile on it, so I rushed to grab the baby from her arms. It was in that moment that I smelled the vodka on her breath. Yep, she did get rid of the vodka, but not down the kitchen sink!

My hosts thanked the chief and as he was leaving the Chief said:
"You two sisters, come to the committee tomorrow; I'll get you diapers and formula for the babies without you standing in line! Sepehr could have been very angry with me, but he was such a nice and considerate guy who never mentioned that incident to me again. I was physically and mentally exhausted and couldn't stand on my feet any longer. I needed to shower and clean up all the sweat and sticky milk from my body. I nursed Maral after I calmed down a bit and we all went to sleep. I don't think I ever talked to this wonderful couple about that night in detail. I do remember that when we got inside, Sepehr said:
"I'm glad you are okay. I just destroyed one of my paintings as you weren't back. I was, and still am, very embarrassed for what I put them through that night.

Enough is enough!

Next morning, extremely embarrassed and still tired, I was very sure that I wanted to take my children and go to my father's house. I packed our belongings and took a cab to my childhood house. It was a bitter sweet feeling; being "home" was good, but not being sure about the near future was nerve wracking. The comforting relief of being in my childhood home was marred by my constant fear of being taken. My dad's bed and closet were in the front room downstairs, so we installed in his room. It was a mild winter, but I still needed to use some sort of heater for both that room and the large kitchen. Having a toddler, I avoided the portable kerosene heater in the bedroom and found our old large electric heater and used it for our room. We had a large kerosene water heater in the kitchen which needed to be filled up manually, so I needed to purchase some kerosene. We had a large tank in the back-yard for filling up with Kerosene and using as was needed.

I had some money in the bank, but it wasn't much and I knew very well that I had to think of something for our expenses. The bedroom was warm; the hallway was very cold, and the kitchen was slightly warm. So, I was going from the bedroom to the kitchen, facing different temperatures as I went. Every time I wanted to give Amir a bath I had to carry a portable kerosene heater upstairs, warm up the bathroom, take it out, give him a bath, and dress him quickly in the small area outside the bathroom.

After a few days I heard from Polad's friends. They told me that I MUST try to find him. They explained to me that as long as the family tried to find these political prisoners there were fewer chances of the Islamic government killing them under torture. I was guided to go to the local police and file a missing person report, and also claim that he had a large amount of cash on him.

One morning I took the babies and left the house on that mission. Our house was not by the side of a main road so you couldn't find a cab without walking at least a mile to the main intersection. When I was single and younger that walk felt like nothing! I was always a light and fast walker, but not now, with two children, one 2 years old and the other 1 month old. I had to carry baby Maral in one arm, with the bag of diapers, bottles and extra clothes for both, in the same hand, and hold Amir's little hand with the other hand. Amir was a baby as well and walking for a long time was extremely tiring for him. My poor baby would walk for five or six minutes and then would ask me to carry him. I wished that I could carry him all the way, but I couldn't do that for more than fifteen minutes, and then had to put Amir back down to walk. Our little group would take five times longer than a normal person to get to a destination, but what had to be done had to be done.

So that day we walked to the main street and took a cab to the nearest police station. We had to walk again after getting out the cab, and when we entered the police station the baby was crying and Amir looked as if he had just climbed a mountain. The two policemen looked at me, looked at each other, and looked back at me and the children, with sad and concerned looks after I told them my story. I think they knew exactly what was going on, but we all stayed in character! I claimed that he had a large amount of cash on him and had left the house to buy a car and never came back. They took all the information from me to follow up. Then I was told to put an advertisement in Tehran's main newspapers and ask people to look out for my husband. I can't remember if I did that or not. We came back to my dad's house in the same fashion.

The next morning I felt sick. I thought that it was a simple cold and would pass, but Maral started showing symptoms of fever, by crying and not taking the bottle. Then Amir started coughing so badly that I had to sit him up during the night so he could breathe. I was trying not to get anybody involved in my situation, so I refrained from calling any of my old friends who had that phone number for the past ten years or so. Nobody knew where I had gone or who I had married. So, if I didn't contact them they wouldn't try to call our house after all those years.

Eventually, though, I realized that all three of us were very sick and must see a doctor. I gave in and called Fafar, one of my oldest and dearest friends from high school. Fafar didn't have a phone in her apartment, so I called her landlord, who was living on the first floor of the same building, for him to get her. She came through for us like an angel. Fafar's husband took us to the doctor's office. We were all prescribed antibiotics. I had to strictly keep to the correct dosage, every four or six hours, especially for Maral. I developed a horrible cough which lasted for years to come. It was so bad that I would lose control of my bladder and bowel movements! The children started getting better, but somehow I wasn't improving; I was coughing none stop, especially at nights. I would sweat so badly that I had to change my clothing several times during the night.

###

Life was getting semi-normal for us, living and staying under one roof, having food and heat and a phone line. But then, for a few nights I began feeling that we were being watched. Maybe it was that I had a high fever causing my imagination to run riot, or maybe we were under surveillance! Every night I thought that they could come when we were asleep, gang rape me and give my children to Islamic families. I started going to bed with tight jeans and long shirts, so if they did come I would have a chance of being difficult to rape!

Miracle or a very smart set up by Polad?
December 1983

I finally decided to call the US and let my family know what had happened, so I called and told my father that Polad had gone to the University of Tehran "which was always the source of all demonstrations" and I was alone with the children. I knew that my father would get my meaning and he did! He told me that he would be back to be with me and the children as soon as possible.

One day I received a post office card regarding the arrival of a package from the US. I left the children with the Zoroastrian lady neighbor and walked up the street to take a cab to the post office. It was a nice day and I hadn't been up that street in years! The expensive fruit and fish market was still there, and I was remembering my childhood when my mother and I used to walk there for shopping. My dear God! Was that my car parked at the corner of that alley? It couldn't be; no, it wasn't possible; surely it was just a car that looked like mine. I took a few long and fast strides and looked inside the car through the side window… Yes, IT WAS MY CAR! The keys were in it too, but the doors were locked. I was walking around the car with mixed feelings of puzzlement, happiness and sadness.
Where is Polad then?
Why did he leave the car with the keys in it?
He must have known they were waiting for him, so he left the car for me to find… is that it? Is he still alive?
What if he was shot to death as soon as he walked to the place?
Where did he have to go that he parked the car here?

As I was circling the car I saw a shoeshine man who appeared to be in his fifties. He was working in the shade, in front of a large gate that was the opening for a very old large garden. The man was busy moving the polish brush back and forth and singing…" *The innocent one goes to the gallows but will never be hanged, Yeah, the innocent one goes to the gallows but not in the noose*" And he gave me a quick short look as he continued his work. I walked towards him and asked if he had seen the driver of that car, and if so, when? He said:

"A while back, I saw a man who parked this car and walked that way," he pointed to the alley, "but he didn't come back." He looked away from me and started working on the shoe that he was holding. I walked to a key making place and paid someone to open the car door for me. I drove the car to the post office and back to my father's house, wondering how all this could possibly have happened. The next day, I drove to that street again and didn't see the shoeshine man. I tried on numerous occasions after that, but I never saw him again… Finding my car was extremely helpful to me with my two little children… The Universe had come to my aid, yet again.

Another Test for me

There was one room on the second floor in which we had put some of my mom's memorabilia and furniture, and locked the door. There was also a bedroom on the second floor that Polad had used as an office (my childhood room), when we were living there. I knew in my heart that one day they would come for me, so I decided to start cleaning the house of any kind of pictures or documents that could incriminate me. It wasn't easy to do that with two babies and a cold house, but I had to start doing that. Every evening I would feed Maral and put her down for a nap and go to the second floor with Amir. He would be sitting on the floor and I would go through papers...

I couldn't believe the stuff that I found in that room. I knew Polad was a very careful person, so I was extremely shocked when I found car titles in other people's names, pictures of them and their children. If found, that would be a bad situation for Polad. I could get into a lot of hot water too. You see, on my mom's side, I was a Baha'i; that is, a religious minority that the Islamic government was absolutely against. Remember, they killed my aunt and her husband for that very reason. On my dad's side, I could get connected to the Shah and his group due to the fact that he had had a somewhat sensitive job, as the Minister of Education during the previous government. My husband was active in a very strong left-minded political organization.

I had to clean up the house of everything related to any of the above subjects! After cleaning Polad's office, I started with my mom's religious books and burned them all. I buried the Baha'i jewelry. To think that I hadn't been worried about my connection to Auntie Nour and her Baha'i activities! At the time, I had been convinced that they wouldn't "get me" for religious reasons. I was no longer an active Baha'i member. I'd gone to the school for twelve years and gone to youth gatherings, perhaps for two more years, after that, but now I had no connections to the Baha'i organization in any active form. I stated that I would tell the authorities that I was of no religion and that was that. Polad had, on the other hand, been very concerned about my connection with her. He talked of the dangers of being associated with them. Now reality was striking me and panicking me into action.

I then took the large framed pictures of my dad and the Shah and burned them too! It is easy to just say that I "burned" them, but I had to be creative with that too. I used to take these items to the back yard during the early hours of the morning (5 or 6 a.m.) when the flames couldn't be seen. The backyard was off from the kitchen, so I would burn some fried onion or rice on purpose to cover up the smell of burning paper.

One day as I was cleaning Polad's office all day and Amir was playing next to me on the floor, he fell asleep at 7 p.m. It was very strange to see that active child going to sleep so early and on his own. As I picked him up, to carry him into his bed, I realized that he was very warm; he was burning up with a high fever. I brought him to our bedroom on the first floor, and tried to cool him off by wrapping damp sheets around his little body, but it didn't work.

I knew that I had to take him to a hospital, so I called Polad's aunt's house to see if she would help us. She answered the phone and I told her briefly that Polad was gone for a while, and I needed someone to come with me to hold Maral, and help me with the directions to the hospital. She hung up on me! After a few minutes, the phone rang and it was her husband; he said:
"I don't know what you said to my wife, but she has passed out, and if you need help you should contact your own mother and not us!"

Well, my mother and mother-in-law were both in the US, so I had to find someone else for help! The problem was that my family had never had any kind of relationship with the neighbors. Mom never talked to any of them and neither did I. We only said "hello" to the Zoroastrian lady, who had spoken to me the day that I was checking out my old neighborhood.

Unfortunately, she wasn't home that night, so I went to another neighbor. I asked if her husband could please go with us to the hospital. She wasn't happy and wasn't shy in telling me NO! I begged her, and her husband came to the door to see what was holding up his wife. He agreed to go to the hospital with Amir and I, so I begged the woman to please take sleeping Maral until we came back. Boy, was she angry with me, but didn't want to say anything against her husband's wishes. We took my car and drove away.

I was under the impression that Amir had been poisoned by eating something from the floor in that room, while I was busy sorting the papers. So I asked him to take us to the Poison Control Center. I was so glad that he was driving because that hospital was a long way, right in the heart of Tehran. Once we arrived, I carried Amir into the ER; it was a dirty, crowded place with no doctors or nurses in sight! There were white plastic-covered beds and some had urine or blood running on them. I was squeezing my child to my chest, looking around like a wild animal.

A man, with no uniform, approached me, grabbed Amir and put him on a bed with urine on it. Before I could say a word, he checked Amir's pulse and looked in his eyes with a little flash light and said:
"He is too far gone; take him home; there is nothing we can do for him."
I was furious. I couldn't believe that place or what this man was saying. I grabbed my child from that filthy bed and yelled at the so called doctor saying:
"Can't you act and talk like a real doctor? What is wrong with you?" He grabbed a mop that was propped against the wall and began mopping the floor! I screamed at him again and asked:
"Since when do those who mop the piss off the floor check the patients?" He turned towards me, with a wild and aggressive seeming body language, and yelled back at me that I was out of line. At that point my neighbor came to my rescue and told the man that I was under a lot of stress, and he should forgive me! I still don't know if the man was a doctor mopping the floor or a janitor who was pretending to be a doctor…

We left and returned home. I put Amir's hot little body in bed, collected Maral back from the neighbor, and sat on the floor, feeling as helpless as I could ever remember feeling before. I think the man had spoken to his wife about my situation, because she and two other women from the neighborhood came to the house that night, and quietly sat on the floor to give me some emotional support. Around midnight, I asked them to leave. All night I was sitting looking at Amir and the clock…

Around 7 a.m. I called Amir's pediatrician's house. This man was an angel; he was in his sixties and had studied in France. His French wife answered the phone, and with a very cute accent talked to me in Farsi. She said that the doctor had already left his house for his office and should arrive there around 8 a.m. I had to wait another hour, which felt like another day to me. I carried the babies, one by one, into the car that I had parked inside our yard, grabbed everything, and drove to the doctor's office about ten minutes away.

Upon arrival there, I wouldn't leave one of them alone in the car, even for two minutes, to carry the other one in; so I had to carry both of them in, one in each arm to walk into the office. As soon as the doctor saw me, he took two long strides towards us and grabbed Amir from my right arm. "Get in, get in!" he repeated. He put Amir on the examination table and checked him for a good ten minutes or so...

He wanted to know when his fever had started. I said that it was at 7 p.m. the previous night that I had noticed it. He asked some other questions to see if he was coughing or had diarrhea or a runny nose. My answer was negative to all of his questions, so he took a deep breath, turned to me, with his hand softly on Amir's body, and said:
"I can't find anything wrong with him and I can't believe that the hospital didn't admit him last night."

I looked at Amir's little body and his big eyes that were still closed. His long eyelashes were so pretty, as if someone had put makeup on them. His little cheeks were red and he hadn't drunk or eaten anything since 5 p.m. the evening before. The doctor continued with:
"It is either a twenty-four hour virus or Meningitis. Take him home and watch him closely; if you see his lips turning blue and it seems like he cannot breathe, you need to get him to the hospital in a matter of minutes."

I brought the children back home and waited and waited...Women neighbors showed up in the afternoon and sat on the floor in that room. Little Maral was normal; I was feeding her every few hours and changing her diaper. Those people coming over was such a great support for me, because I had no energy to play or talk with Maral when she was awake and they were taking care of that for me. She was a very cute baby with a very little face, nose and lips, but huge eyes!

Time was passing very slowly... That day took forever to become afternoon and the sun was so lazy in going down... I spent the day sitting next to Amir, trying to cool off his little body with damp cloths. The clock turned to 7 p.m. Amir opened his eyes and said "Mama -- bottle"!

The women cheered! I picked him up and kissed him, kissed him, and kissed him some more... it was as if a miracle had happened in that room. Some of the women claimed that it was an answer and thanks to their prayers that he recovered... I didn't care what they thought; I was just so happy that my little boy was alive and well.

Home Sweet home

After that night I started to mingle with the neighbors a little. I realized my extreme need to be able to count on *somebody* and here they were living a few feet away from me. During the nice evenings the neighbors would open their front doors and talk to each other, while their young children were riding their bikes or playing around the alley. I decided to join them and it was a pleasant addition to my life! I liked it and doing that gave me a feeling of "belonging" and not such abandonment.

When I was growing up in that very house, we weren't allowed to play in the alley; we were told that we weren't "alley kids" and playing in the alley was beneath our class. Oh well…time had passed and things had changed a lot for me, so I continued getting to know my neighbors, after having lived next to them for the past twenty years!

The money in my bank account was going down and I had no source of income. My solution was to sell a few items from the house, but they belonged to my mother, and not me. I called her and she said that she would never come back to live in Iran, so I could sell some dishes or her clothing to pay for food, kerosene and gasoline for my car. Having my car back helped me to socialize with some friends and family, and put some normality in my life. I drove to nearby towns to see people and it was always fun to be able to get out of the house and go places with my children.

Sometimes I received messages from Polad's friends who were telling me to get in touch with them. They were those with whom I really had had no bonds, so I wasn't sure if they really wanted to see me, or if they were trying to find out if I had their phone numbers and addresses! Not only was I in the habit of living in suspicion, but everybody was so concerned about their own safety and the possibility that I would be followed to their homes. In my suspicion, I would always say:

"I was always told by Polad to close my eyes while he was driving to members of the organization's houses, so I don't know where they live." This was true anyway, as far as many of them were concerned.

The season was changing and the children and I couldn't just live with the clothes that I had packed that night before leaving our apartment. I decided to just go back to my place and live as normally as possible. I had a feeling that they wouldn't come after us in that apartment building, because Polad had taken us out that night and he was not captured from there. I just needed to go back home and I did! Although I had no phone line in there, it was so good to go back home and feel safe and secure within my own place. However, there was one problem…

I was never involved in Polad's arrangements with the landlord. I didn't even know the man and had no phone numbers for contacting him. The apartment building was large. It was four stories high with four units on each floor.

Numb

My two little angels two years after Polad was gone. They are playing in the little porch of our apartment.

After I moved back to the apartment my father came back from the US and stayed with us for a while. Amir and Maral bonded with him really rapidly, and that was like winning a lottery of a couple of millions! It was so satisfying, seeing them with their grandpa. He was a gentle, loving grandpa who took care of my children with so much love and consideration.

During that time I signed up for typing class in both Farsi and English. I would leave the children with my dad for about two hours to go to the class. Dad would make up and give the bottle to Maral and play with Amir until I came back home from my daily class. He also had his personal life and would leave us for a few days at a time, which didn't bother me. Actually, I liked it because I could visit my friends and invite them over to have a few drinks and listen to music. Did I say "drinks"? Well, there were no alcoholic beverages allowed in Islamic Iran, so that is a different story which I'll get to later!

In my apartment building, there was one family on the same floor with whom I felt kind of comfortable -- a young couple with a 4 or 5 year old boy. I had seen the woman going to work and I knew she was a nurse. When Maral needed Penicillin shots I had asked this woman to come over to give her the injection. There was something familiar about them; the way the husband looked and the way they carried themselves was just like Polad and his friends! I was sure they belonged to some political group, but I didn't know which one.

I asked them to please tell the landlord that he needed to deal with me for the monthly rent which was $50,000 IRR per month (about $450). The landlord wanted to see me, so we arranged a meeting at my apartment. I asked my dad to please be there that day. The landlord showed up and said:

"I don't like dealing with single women; you must leave!" He wouldn't change his mind and really wanted us out of there. Finally, my father signed the lease and rented the apartment under his name. Somehow I have no memory of how I paid him the rent. I think that he probably gave me bank account information, because I don't remember seeing him ever again... I had enough money left to pay the rent for one more month, so I had to quickly come up with a plan.

I had my mother's and sister's food coupons from the childhood house area, so at least once a week, I would get in my car and drive to that area for forty-five minutes to do the food shopping. It was great that I had their share too; that helped me a lot in getting more meat, eggs, soap and other products.

My good old car was faithfully taking care of us until one morning, while I was in my old neighborhood -- as I tried to start the car it caught on fire! I saw the smoke coming out of the hood, so silly me popped the hood open to see what was going on. Of course, as soon as I did that the oxygen augmented the flames! Before I knew what was happening, an army soldier showed up holding a blanket, and he threw the blanket on the fire and shut the hood! It had happened so fast that I was still standing there, in surprise, watching him. He told me not to try to start the car and to take a cab.

I knew a mechanic up the street; I walked there and I asked him to fix the car for me. Then I took a cab and came home with all the groceries that I was holding in both hands. I was so glad that my dad was home with the children and I didn't have them with me.

My dad returned to the US after staying with us for two more weeks, and as always, we asked him to please stay with the family in the US and not to come back to Iran. This game was played between all of us against him for twenty years! He would travel between the two countries to keep his Green Card situation in order. We would ask him to please stay in the US this time and he wouldn't give us a straight answer. After two months or so, he would "escape" from the house in the US to come back to Iran, to see me and the children and his other woman.

Chapter Twelve

Where is My Husband?

January 1984

I was told by Polad's friends that there was a man named "Haj Agha Rabiyee" who was acting as a liaison between the Islamic police (Pasdars) and the regular Police in Iran. I was told that as about four months had passed from the night that Polad had disappeared, this man could help me to locate him. Haj Agha Rabiyee's office was in my old neighborhood, right next to my old high school! That part of Tehran was an area known as 'The Traffic Zone'.

The Traffic Zone was Tehran's business center that used to get extremely tangled up with traffic jams. They found a solution for that problem which was not to allow any personal cars into that area between 6 a.m. and 5 p.m. during work days. Work days in Iran start from Saturday and end on Thursday afternoon, Friday is the weekend. Knowing how busy these kind of people would get I needed to be one of the first ones in the queue to see him, so I had to be able to enter the Traffic Zone before 6 a.m.!

My apartment was on the other side of Tehran, so it would have been very hard for me with two very young children to do that. I decided to contact my cousin, who had a house within the Traffic Zone, to ask her to let us stay there the night before. She accepted and we spent the night in one of her rooms. I seem to remember there was a Kerosene crisis at that time because I remember that room was very cold, and I had to put on the children's winter outerwear, and hold them in my arms all night so they were warm enough.

The next morning we left early and arrived in front of that building at 6:30 a.m. The doors were closed and nobody was there yet. I parked the car right in front, turned up the heat and all three of us took a nice warm deep nap until 8 a.m.! I was woken up by an annoying knock on my car window. I opened my eyes and saw a very concerned woman, bending over looking inside the car and I could hear her saying:
"What a deep sleep they are all in!" I cracked the window and said that we were okay. She said that she was concerned that our car would start rolling down the hill while we were asleep in there. After assuring her that

everything was alright, I looked at the clock. It was time, so I turned off the engine, grabbed the babies and went inside.

Amir was sleepy and tired so he was crying and didn't want to take one more step. He was practically hanging from me. Maral was still sleeping, wrapped in a white thick blanket in my left arm, and I was concerned that Amir's screams would wake her up, but there was nothing I could do! We entered the man's office like a hurricane, with a screaming child, tired and young mother holding an infant in one arm while dragging the other one behind... What a scene, I thought!

"Haj Agha" was talking to some other people when we walked in. He turned his face towards us and told the other people:
"Look at this one; now *she* deserves some attention and not you guys!"

He told a woman-pasdar to take the baby from my arm, but I refused and asked for a chair, so I could sit and hold both children on my knees. They offered me a large chair; I sat down and pulled Amir up on my knee. He put his head on my chest and started playing with Maral's blanket. I told the man about my missing husband. He asked if I had reported him missing, and I confirmed that I had. Then he asked for Polad's full name and his father's full name. He picked up the phone and called the "Evin Prison".

It seemed that he was pretty 'buddy, buddy' with them and that scared me. I thought "He can't be on my side if he is so friendly with these animals." I maintained a cool exterior and tried to show no feelings. My plan was that he wouldn't lie to me based on my facial reaction to his conversation. He quickly asked for my husband's name, last name and his father's full name. Then he asked me for the date of his disappearance and repeated it to them.

He paused and listened to the person on the phone. He was saying: "Aha, yep, aha, okay then" and then he hung up the phone. Despite my cool exterior, I felt like screaming at him. He looked at me with confidence. He said;
"Were you aware of your husband's political activities?"
I looked at him straight in the eyes and said:
"Political what?"

He leaned forward on his big, wide desk, putting his hands together, tilted his head a bit and repeated the question. I looked straight at him and said:
"Haj Agha, I don't know anything about such matters."
At that point he said:
"Then why are you here asking for my help?"
"I went to the Police Office located in Kahk SQ, when he first disappeared, and filed a report," I answered. "That was a few months ago, and then I heard from some neighbors that, if he is not dead on the side of a road somewhere, you may be able to find his whereabouts. They said that

there are some people who have been captured during street demonstrations, whose names haven't been published yet, and you have the authority to get to those names."

He appeared to believe me and yet he asked:
"Street demonstrations? Why would he be doing that?"
"Well, Haj Agha, who isn't doing that these days? Everybody goes out to see what is going on in the streets, and some get captured just for being in the wrong place at the wrong time," I answered.
Sitting back, he said:
"Your husband is in Evin prison. You must call them first to see what day of the month is the visiting day."
He wrote the phone number on a piece of paper and handed it to me. We had known all along that if he was not killed at the time of his capture, he would be at Evin, but this man's confirmation was my key to contacting Evin without being under suspicion myself.

As I didn't have a phone in my apartment, I used to ask at the stores if I could use their phone for some change and they were all very helpful. Finally, I was able to call Evin Prison and, after being on hold for a long time and getting disconnected several times, I was told that he was there and I could go to a former amusement park for a visit on a certain date.

It was three months after my visit to Haj Agha Rabiyee when I was told to go to Evin to see Polad. One morning, I put the children in the car and drove to the area. I remember being on the highway that I used to drive on to go to college, but I couldn't find this place. I drove around the vicinity, back and forth, several times with no luck. Finally, at a red light, I rolled down my window and asked a man who was in the car next to me. He looked at the children on the back seat, shook his head with sadness and concern, and gave me directions to get there.

When we finally arrived I saw a very large group of people walking in different directions. Some were crying; some were standing in queues in front of the little office windows where you used to buy the amusement park tickets. All the queues were long, so it wouldn't really make any difference which one I chose. I picked one and stood there as patiently as possible with the babies. After one hour I reached the little window and gave Polad's name. The guy told me that based on Polad's last name I was in the wrong queue and I had to go to another window! Amir was not very happy about all the standing and Maral was waking up in my arms and needed to be changed. I stood in the other queue and finally arrived at the window. I gave them Polad's full name and after looking through some papers they told me that he wasn't there!

It was April of 1984. The weather was getting warm and I wasn't really comfortable in that full Islamic head cover, long pants and long black uniform I was wearing. I told them that Haj Agha Rabiyee had told me that he was there. They didn't like that at all and almost screamed at me:

"Who the heck does this man think he is, interfering with the regulations like that?"

They asked for my full name and address and told me to call them after a week or so to see if he was transferred there or not. I had no choice but to leave that day and bring my exhausted children back home.

I kept calling them from the stores until one month later, in May they told me that he was there and I could go back to that park to board the visitor's bus to Evin Prison.

Chapter Thirteen

Surviving...

The Yard Sale -- February 1984

I was living in an apartment with a rent of approximately $450 per month. On the other hand, our large old house was there and my mother had told me that she would only come back to sell it and not to live in it. I asked my cousin to help me move all the books from inside to the storage room on the flat roof of the house. As no personal cars were allowed to drive into the Traffic Zone, I would grab the children and take a cab to the house, to move things around. I set up the three large rooms on the first floor for a "household sale".

My mother had already sold all the large and beautiful handmade Persian rugs and had taken the money with her. What I was selling were some female clothes, dishes and some furniture. The formal living and dining room French furniture were excluded! I put an advert in our local newspaper and put some flyers around the neighborhood, called some family and friends and the sale started!

I took the children in the car and we went to the house on a Friday morning for people to come to buy the items. At first I was carrying Maral in my arm and talking to people about the items that they wanted, but I soon realized that I needed both my arms to work with my 'mini market'. I remembered that years ago, when we traveled to the North West of Iran, the gypsies were carrying their babies by wrapping them on their back, so why couldn't I do that? I ran upstairs into my mother's sewing room and found a square soft sheet. I folded it like a triangle, put the baby on the table, backed myself towards the table and wrapped her on my back!

During the day I found better ways to hold her in the position that I wanted, by crossing the wrap on my chest. It was a brilliant idea especially as I had lost some weight, and was back to my old one hundred and ten pounds, and the sheet could be wrapped nice and tight on me. The sale was very successful and I was able to put 200,000 IRR (around $2000) in the bank.

Amir was 3 years old and he had started asking questions, like why Dad didn't come home with us? Why didn't we have any family except

Grandpa? Why did other kids have aunts, uncles and cousins but we didn't?

I was noticing that due to my emotional problems, the children weren't happy either. I knew that I had to do something, so I signed them up in a daycare center. I would drive them there early in the morning and pick them up around 3 p.m. It was really good for both of them to be with other children and some other adults and also good for me to have some time to myself.

March 1984 – NuRooz, The Iranian New Year

The first day of spring (March 20th or 21st) is the Iranian New Year, known as "NuRooz". This date has been celebrated for thousands of years in that part of the Middle East. Ironically, I was in my childhood house for this holiday without any of my family members. I remembered that my mother used to plant pansies in the yard and purchase tulips and hyacinth plants for inside the rooms. All of us children would get new clothing and new shoes for Iranian New year. My father would take us to see his mother and my mom's older sister on the first day of NuRooz.

I had absolutely nothing for NuRooz that year. No family and nobody to share it with, so I decided to take the children on a trip to a friend's house in Mashhad. One of Polad's friends was married to this beautiful very light-skinned woman with large green eyes named Zahra. I knew that the man had been captured just like Polad. I knew Zahra was about to go to Mashhad to visit her family for the holidays, so I bought airplane tickets and went there for a week. What a big mistake! Zahra was very nice, but her family really wasn't much interested in having me and my children there. I realized after two days of being there, but there wasn't much I could do. At the end of the week I came back home and never saw them ever again!

Zahra, on the other hand, kept in touch with me for a while after that trip. When I was trying to empty my dad's house of all its furniture, Zahra asked if she could have my parents' very old bedroom set. I couldn't believe that anybody would want those heavy old pieces, so I happily accepted to give her anything from my dad's house that she could use. A while later, I was invited to their little apartment, and when I arrived I saw my dad's bedroom set in a warm bright room. The room looked good and had a happy atmosphere, and it made me very glad to see the furniture being used in a good way. I told Zahra it was so nice to see something that used to be ours being used and cared for by others. I believe her husband had already been released at that time and she was expecting their first child.

I had sold everything from my parent's house except for the formal living room furniture, including the dining room set, which I arranged to be carried to one of the bedrooms on the second floor. When I unlocked that room's door for the movers to put in the furniture, I saw a lot of items that I didn't recognize! There were a few large suit cases, coffee table, chairs, and some boxes with kitchen items in them. I had no idea whose stuff was stored in my dad's house. Fortunately, there was enough room to store the other items from the formal living room.

I decided to rent the large house and live on the rent money. So, I put an advert in the newspaper and gave my cousin's home phone number. They received a lot of phone calls and I had to show the house to a few people. One day, when I was picking up the children from the daycare center, one of the owners asked me if I still had the house available for renting, for the daycare center.

We all thought that it was such a wonderful idea! We knew them and a few of our friends had their children in their care every day. I asked for 3000,000 IRR (I think one Dollar was about 100 IRR at that time) security deposit and 200,000 IRR rent per month. There were three women who were sharing the business, and during the time of moving the daycare to my dad's house, one of them went her separate way.

The other two women came to the house and thoroughly loved the place, but there was one problem; the house was heated with individual large kerosene heaters with wide metal chimneys, through one wall of each room. Having those hot dinosaurs wouldn't be safe with a bunch of toddlers running around. Farzaneh was one of the two women with whom I signed the contract. She came up with a solution. She told me that she would pay for the house to have a hot water heating system installed. It would cost a total of 1000,000 IRR so she would pay me less than our agreed upon rent per month until that total would be achieved by her and afterwards the actual monthly rent would be paid. We wrote everything down and signed.

I was very happy; I had come up with an attractive income within a few months after my husband was taken away from us. I put the security deposit of 3000,000 IRR (approximately $ 30,000) in a bank. The funny part was that she charged me the normal monthly amount per child for Amir and Maral to go there even though she was renting the house from me. I agreed, based on the fact that business is business; she was paying and I had to do the same.

This is my little Maral taking her very first steps. I was able to send this picture to Polad when he was in Evin Prison.

Life became so good for the children and me with that income! I would drop them off in the morning, go back to the apartment, do some housework and then would go to a salon and have a nice massage every other day! I had no problem sending money and clothing into the jail for Polad either. Although my financial problem was resolved, I had emotionally good and bad days. I used to keep myself and the children busy on a daily schedule. Every day after coming home from the daycare center I would give them a notebook and a few coloring pencils to do their 'homework'! I thought that doing so would give them the habit of doing work at home after school. They would draw or just put some lines on the page and I would ask them what they had learned that day...

Sometimes I was very happy and care free and sometimes not so much. I would cry a lot in the privacy of my home, without being able to name the reason. Physically, I was getting sick a lot. My old chronic cough was back in full force. I would cough until I gagged or would actually throw up. Irritable bowel movement was added to my problems! It was horrible; I had to control the desperate need to use the bathroom, while I was standing in line for prison visiting, or when I was trying to put down a crying or sick child for a nap. The other problems that immerged were my skin allergies. Round red, puffy, watery and extremely itchy spots appeared on my legs and the back of my hands. I tried all kinds of skin creams or medicine with no results. I purchased cortisone cream; that would only make the itch go away temporarily, and as a result of using cortisone, black hair started growing on the back of my hands which was very ugly!

After a month or so, one of Polad's old friends sent me a message asking if I would agree to lend their organization the security money that I had received from my tenant, and they would pay it back to me as soon as I asked for it. I agreed and lent them the money without getting anything in writing from them.

Chapter Fourteen
Thirty Six Questions and Counting...
April of 1984

My dad came back and stayed with us at my apartment. I had a regular single bed right next to the apartment door for Amir and a baby bed with high railings for Maral. When my dad joined us, I got rid of the baby bed, let my dad use Amir's bed, and ordered a bed from the carpenter downstairs, for both the children. I designed this bed to be a high railing baby bed on top with a large drawer underneath it, with a thick mattress. At night the drawer could be drawn out to be Amir's bed, and would go back in during the day. I drew all the pieces with dimensions marked on their sides and gave it to the carpenter to build at a cost of 70,000 IRR (around USD 700). He loved it and not only built one for me, but made a few more and sold them!

Finally, after making daily phone calls to the authorities, we were given the visiting day at Evin prison. I informed my dad and he told an old friend. This old friend was my orthodontist when I was 16 years old! I remember that he was in his mid-thirties and I had such a crush on him. He was a very charismatic man with black colored eyes. He wasn't very tall, but very much in shape. He was the son of one of the very powerful tribes of North West Iran. I don't know much about his background -- just that he used to live with his mother and his nanny from his childhood!

The nanny was a very tall and beautiful woman who loved him as if he was hers. She would take care of the house, cooking and cleaning. The nanny's name was "Ahoo" which means Deer in Farsi. She used to dress as if they were still living with the tribe -- all black long clothing with the black headband. His mother however used to dress like the westerners.

Dr. Khan's office was actually the first floor of his residence. I knew that he cared for me and probably wouldn't mind marrying me, if I hadn't been a Baha'i. But I also knew that due to the huge age difference between us, my family would never have accepted such a union. He would travel to Europe several times a year to take part in latest medical conferences regarding his profession. He was a total artist who could do facial surgeries also. When I was his patient he told me that I had one of the rare classical beautiful faces in the world, and asked me if I would mind him making a mold of my face. I agreed and he made it!

As far as I was concerned, I had an over large forehead, fizzy hair, long nose and slightly pushed out chin, which my mother used to call a sign of my stubbornness! He had that copy of my face in his office for years. He used to say that people asked him who the beautiful model was! He called me shortly after my engagement to Polad and told me to collect it from him.

My dad told me that we needed to see Doctor Khan before going to Evin Prison. He explained to me that this doctor had many influential patients/friends and could help me safely come back out, after walking into Evin to see Polad. So, one evening my dad and I took the children along with us to see the doctor. It was a strange feeling. The office was the same, and I remembered walking in there on hot summer days, and he would bring watermelon slices, telling me that I should rehydrate myself after walking from my house to his office on those hot summer days.

It was about ten years later… and here I was with two little children, in the same building. He had a few patients in the waiting room, so we sat down and waited. I also remembered thinking that he didn't have many patients back then, because his waiting room was always empty; then the thought struck me that maybe he would purposely schedule me that way! As we were waiting Maral woke up and began crying and fussing, so I walked outside in the yard to avoid bothering the other patients. I was walking in his yard, swaying the baby in my arms knowing that the doctor was watching me through his office window. I recalled the day when he had tried to kiss me on the lips, and I slapped him not once, but twice on both sides of his face and ran outside. He ran after me saying:
"Please come back inside… I don't want you to leave like this..."
Wow, it seemed to be a hundred years ago…

Maral became quiet, I went back inside and the doctor walked into the waiting room and asked us to follow him into his office. He is mad at me, I thought to myself. He didn't smile and was talking down to me. He said to be truthful and learn the daily Islamic prayer for God's sake! He also said to learn the names of the authorities in the government, as a sign of following the Islamic government's progress. He showed no interest in my beautiful children and didn't even ask their names. He asked for my phone number to get back to me with more information regarding *the* day. As I didn't have a phone we decided that I would call him.

I think it was two or three days later when around 8 or 9 p.m. I drove, with the children, to a public phone booth a long way from my apartment. Maral was asleep in her car-seat, but Amir jumped out of the car and started playing around the booth. Dr. Khan was as cold as before and told me that I would be interviewed by a man named "Brother Abbass" at the Evin building. I repeated the name and he loudly said:

"I would appreciate it if you didn't loudly repeat in the street what I'm saying." He also repeated that I had to seem interested in the Islamic government's decisions and progress...

Visiting day arrived. My dad was with us. I had been told to be there very early in the morning. My mind was in turmoil -- I had mixed feelings. There was the excitement of seeing Polad, but I was also so scared of going there. Without telling my dad, I made a list of what children need or eat, and left it on the washer and dryer in the kitchen, just in case I didn't return. We left around 6 a.m. that day with the children in tow. We arrived at the park in good time. As my dad was not Polad's family he had to stay at the park pickup point, but the children and I took the second bus to Evin...

I was sitting in the bus squeezing my children to my chest. I was so frightened, going there with them, but I had to do what I had to do. So, summoning all my courage, I got down from the bus twenty minutes later, when we finally arrived there. We were guided to the building to stand in line to give our names and information. After that we were left in a large room waiting for our names to be called... By the time they called my name, it was 11 o'clock. They body-searched me and the babies, then guided us into a large area with individual kiosks with glass and a phone next to each one. I had difficulty breathing; I was so excited to see Polad alive.

He was already standing behind the glass when we got to his kiosk. My God, he had lost at least fifty pounds. Forcing myself to be strong, I smiled at him as I picked up Amir and put him on the counter, so that Polad could see him. Maral was in my arms. Polad indicated the phone receiver. When I picked up the phone he said:
"Are you okay? Look at HER," he smiled and pointed to Maral.

We chatted a little, but we both knew that we really couldn't 'talk'. Then he said:
"Do you want to send them in so I can hold them?"
Although feeling desperately reluctant to hand over my children, I realized how much Polad must have been waiting for that moment. So I said:
"Sure, of course."
He called the guard and he was told to wait until after the visit for that. After ten or fifteen minutes we were told that the visit was over. At that point women were giving their children to the guards to take inside, so they could have 'in person' time with their fathers. I did the same. Guards then guided us out to wait for our children to be returned to us.

After twenty minutes or so, the door opened and children started walking back to their mothers. Guards were carrying the younger ones, and as Maral couldn't walk yet, I was staring at the door waiting to see who was bringing her and Amir back to me. I hated this, but I knew how important it was for Polad to see, kiss and hold his children. At last, here was my Maral in a guard's arms, screaming with what seemed like all her might. Amir was walking trying to keep up with the man who was holding Maral. I grabbed them both and held them tight. According to Amir, Maral was crying because the man hit her head on the wall. Ah, the tiger in me could have killed that guy in that instant!

We were guided through the same walkway we had entered by, to get back to the buses to return to the park, where my dad had been waiting all day for us to come home. We had almost made it outside when they called out my name and ordered me to stay for questioning. It was around 2 p.m. I was tired, the children were tired and hungry, but I had no choice but to wait to see what they wanted...

They took their time and the last group boarded the bus. The heavy iron door was closing and I noticed a few birds pecking on the dirt in the sun.

"Maybe this is the last time I will see that view," I thought as I took in every detail... everything seemed to be in slow motion as the door was closing and the view was disappearing. The heavy closing door cast a shadow over the view and then the door was shut tight...

Walking away from the tall petrifying Evin's wall with the 2 babies on hand, after missing the visitors' bus, going back to where all the cars were parked.

There I was standing in front of a young man who was sitting at a metal desk with some papers in front of him.

"Give your kids to a family member for a while; we only need you," he said.

"I don't have anybody here; my father is at the park," I answered.

He was evidently very unhappy with that, but controlled himself and gave me a crooked smile which ran shivers up and down my spine.

"Sit down," he said.

I sat down with both children one in my arms and the other on my lap. Maral was asleep and Amir was too scared to act up. Poor boy could probably feel my fear as well. There were thirty six written questions and they wanted details for every one of them. Okay, I thought; the sooner I start, the faster I'll get to go home.

The first few were about my information, my address and family members that I was living with. The rest were about people with whom my husband was socializing. They wanted names and if not known, descriptions. I wrote down something like this for all of those questions:

"My husband is a very traditional Iranian man. He never allowed me to see or talk to his friends. He was rarely home himself so I really haven't seen many of his friends in our house. If anybody knocks at the door he orders me to go to the other room and stay there until they are gone. I have been a very obedient wife and never wanted to make him angry".

Of Course, this wasn't strictly true, but it was the only way I could get them off my back. I had always been a good writer so getting through the whole questionnaire didn't take me more than ten to fifteen minutes.

This young man introduced himself as "Brother Abbass". I found out later that they all called themselves that! He was actually a clean shaved, small young man and didn't look like an Islamic Pasdar at all. If I had seen him in a demonstration, I would have thought he was a member of some communist group.

They finally let me out! I couldn't believe that it was over until the gray iron door had been opened and here we were outside on a warm sunny day in Tehran. Upon looking around, I discovered that all the buses were gone. The dusty road was abandoned…so I held Maral and the bag of children's kit in one hand and took little Amir's hand with the other and began the slow, long walk back to the park, knowing that the walk would take us at least one and a half hours…

As we were nearing the park, my dad saw us from a distance. He began running towards us, but was forced to change to fast walking and limping. Dad picked up Amir who was screaming at that point. As we stood face to face, I could see that my old dad had been crying and I felt really bad for him. In a broken voice he said:

"I saw all the buses come and go and you weren't on any of them. I didn't know if I should drive up to the prison or wait here."

When we came back home it was around 6 p.m. Visiting was once or twice a month, but that was the only time that they held me for questioning. Polad and I could also write letters to each other on a short form. The prisoners' families were responsible for sending them money for food and blankets to sleep. Everybody was also sending clothes to their captured loved ones. Polad asked me for a Farsi to English dictionary, which I took with me on the next visit, but they wouldn't take it from me, saying that only Farsi books were allowed.

Normally I would get to see Polad every two weeks unless something had changed. It always meant getting up around 4 a.m., getting the children ready, pack diapers and bottles, extra clothing for them just in case, some bread and cheese, and a gallon of water to wash hands or the baby's bottom if necessary. Getting everything down into the car from the fourth floor was always very tiring and time consuming. Depending on which building he was being held at, we would have between one or two hours driving time ahead of us.

One time when we arrived at the amusement park, to board the bus to Evin Prison, I saw a young woman who was walking along the fence, reaching her arm up, touching the fence slightly with her fingers as she was walking back and forth. Her eyes were glazed. She looked as if she was in excruciating pain, but you couldn't tell where in her body was hurting. Her head was tilted to one side and her hair cover was pulled a little back; I could see her dark shiny hair. She was looking at people, but I doubt she could see anything or anybody. It was spring time and the weather was beautiful, but seeing her would have brought anyone down to the reality that you weren't there to enjoy the weather.

A few people were standing close to her and just watching her walking and touching the fence. I grabbed Amir's hand and walked slowly towards them. I purposely wanted to get close to them without arousing anybody's attention. Finally, here I was within two feet of one of the men and asked him:

"Do you know her?"

He nodded his head.

"What's wrong?" I asked.

"We came here for the regular visit to my brother, who is her husband, but when we got in front of the window to find out what time we should get on the bus to Evin, they told us that he was executed a few days ago," he quietly answered.

I felt as if someone had dumped a huge bucket of ice on my head. I looked at the woman and looked at the man again. I told him:

"I'm very sorry for you, but why aren't you guys leaving?"

"Because she doesn't believe it, and keeps asking them where he has been transferred to…"

I will never forget that day and the woman's face. It was something that I feared at every visiting time. Had he been executed? Had he been tortured and did he look really beaten up, so they would tell me that he had been transferred?

Kiss Daddy Goodnight…

During one visit, Polad silently moved his lips to mouth the word "razor" and pointed at his face. He wanted to shave. You see, not shaving is one of the signs of being a traditional Muslim, and these young prisoners would do anything to avoid giving the Pasdars any satisfaction. Back then you could buy a pack of ten razor blades that were wrapped individually. I bought two packs and after taking them out of the box threw them in Amir's plastic boot along with a tooth-brush in his other boot. He was about 3 years old. I whispered in his ear:
"Walk normally and don't look at your boots. Daddy needs this stuff and if the 'bad guys' find out, they won't let us see Daddy again. He looked at me and nodded his head in affirmation, and walked straight towards the door to go through to see his dad. Maral was only one, but she could walk and Amir was holding her hand, guiding her to see Polad. A few minutes later I saw Polad, through the thick glass, pick them up with a big smile. I immediately mouthed "boots" and pointed at Amir. Polad nodded and when the children came back I noticed that Polad had taken all the items!

I used to make pajamas with large pockets and send them in for him, with sweaters, blankets and other items that he needed. I'm sure I was allowed to send in a tooth brush, but maybe he wanted it for someone else who didn't have a visitor. I just don't recall why I secretly sent the tooth brush in like that.

After a while, Polad was moved from Evin to Rajayee Shahr Prison, which was outside Tehran. We would go to the address, which was a large house with many rooms, the owner of which had most likely been killed for being Baha'i or connected to the Shah's government or being politically active or any other ridiculous reason they were very good at coming up with. While in the house, they would ask everyone to line up so they could body search us and give us numbers for the visit.

The atmosphere around Rajayee Shahr Prison was lighter. People would talk and smile more often. I'm not sure why; maybe everybody was under the impression that all the executions were only being done at Evin. One day we were waiting in the yard and I saw a woman wrapping a wide wool scarf around her 10 year old daughter's waist. She pulled the child's sweater over it after she was done. Mom and child were looking around and giggling. I asked another woman next to me what that was about. She said that the jail building was very cold at Gohardasht, and most likely the woman was sending the scarf to her husband via the child.

###

It was about one year after Polad had been taken away from us. Amir was 3 and Maral was 1 year old. We were still in my apartment and my father would travel between my place, his woman and the U.S. I was getting used to my new life -- going for visits, taking care of my children and sometimes going to see friends such as Sepehr and Parvin. I would go to Farsi and English typing classes when my father was home and could stay with the children. I used to cry a lot for no reason. Once, I was washing the dishes and the tears just decided to flow. I could do nothing to stop them. Amir asked:

"Mom, why are you crying?"

"My head hurts, honey. It'll get better..." I answered, trying to smile for him.

I couldn't face my sorrow and fears for Polad and continue my life at the same time. Every cold night I would think about him. I couldn't get to sleep thinking about if he was warm enough. What was happening to him? What were they doing to him? How was he feeling, knowing what was around him? How was he going through the minutes and hours of the day knowing and hearing someone he knew was being tortured and perhaps killed? Did they make them watch their friends' executions? He must have felt extremely lonely during those seven months when I couldn't find him. (Later on I found out that he was being beaten every day, with his eyes wrapped). I had no other choice than to stop "feeling" at all or I wouldn't be able to go on. I just remained passionate towards my children; other than that I had no other emotional connection to anything or anybody.

Maral was a very beautiful baby girl. Mine and Polad's family used to send very pretty clothing and colorful stuff for my children. I was very concerned about Maral being touched inappropriately by the people who took the children to see their parents, so I would always put a pair of long pants on her, even when she was wearing a dress! Despite me doing that I couldn't tolerate the way some of those Islamic men and women used to look at her. They would pinch her cheek and say how cute she was. I had the same problem with Amir too. They would come around him, talking with him in a friendly manner – and that would drive me to distraction.

One day back in September 1985, when we were waiting in line for the visit, a Pasdar walked towards us and handed Maral a single small wild flower and smiled. I immediately grabbed the flower from her, threw it away and told him:

"We don't need your flower."

He looked at me with an expression as if he was saying "Whatever...we have your loved one and you are in our hands" and walked away with a nasty smile. That day passed, and the next time we went there the same Pasdar and a mullah (Muslim religious man) approached me and the

children. It was around noon and we could smell the food all over the building. We had been there since 7 a.m. and had to wait until after the lunch hour to see Polad. The mullah told him:
"Here, give her this," and handed him a piece of paper.
The guy walked over and gave me the paper; it had a number on it.
"What is this for?" I asked.
"Sister, use this number to get yourself and your kids some lunch."
I threw the paper away saying:
"My kids and I will never eat bread from the hands of people like you."
I picked up Maral, took Amir's hand and turned to walk away. As I was doing so I heard the mullah's voice saying: "See, this is what I'm talking about. They don't deserve our kindness."

###

There were a lot of small children in our apartment building. The building's wide porch was used like a yard. Every afternoon, women and children would come to that area; the children would play and the women, wrapped in chadors, would sit in a corner and gossip. I bought two plastic three-wheelers for Amir and Maral, so they could play there too. I would stand in a corner with a book, pretending to read, so that people wouldn't try to talk to me while I was watching my children.

This wasn't possible when it was cold outside, so another way that we would amuse ourselves was to gather in the bedroom, which had a window overlooking the street, and look outside watching the world go by, for a while! There was a bakery directly across the street and we would watch the people who were standing in line to buy fresh bread. The children would be standing on my bed, resting their little arms on the window sill, with me standing next to them. Sometimes I would tell stories about everyone who was standing there and make up names for them! Amir loved that game!

Sometimes while I let them play there a little longer, I would go to the kitchen to make something for dinner, and that was when they would change the game from watching the street to jumping from the window sill onto Mom's bed! During one of those times Maral bit her lip as she jumped and we finished up in the emergency room!

At about 8 p.m. I would tell them to kiss Daddy's picture to say goodnight to him, and then go to bed. I would then leave the music on for them and turn the lights off, to sit in the living room by myself.

As I continued with our routine and started to have a "normal" life, I noticed some faces around our apartment building which looked familiar. I saw so called 'Brother Abbass' one day, who turned his face away as soon as he noticed that I was looking at him. Great, I thought; are they around here to see whom I'm socializing with or are they chasing a young woman who lives alone most of the time? It was a very scary thought, but I had to overcome my fear and be alert about my surroundings, to keep my children and myself as safe as possible. I saw some other Pasdars around the building who I recognized either at the Park or Evin prison during my visits.

Firstly, I made sure the apartment curtains were thick enough to give me privacy, and secondly, I made sure not to dress provocatively, even when I was alone in my own place. I put a chador next to the entrance door, to be able to cover myself every time there was a knock at the door. Summer was coming and I had no air conditioning in the apartment. I used to wear tank-tops with jeans at home so the chador was a good cover to have by the door.

I didn't have anything 'illegal' inside my apartment, but I was still fearful of them getting inside my place when I wasn't home. I would place a strand of my hair covering the front door and the frame every time we left the apartment. That would let me know if there was perhaps somebody inside waiting for me and the children when we returned.

I eventually stopped visiting Polad's friends. One friend was married to a very sweet woman and they had a little daughter. As far as I was aware that man wasn't actually politically active. I was under the impression that he was just a fan. She was a teacher and they were hardly making ends meet.

I still remember their wedding in the mountains. They both belonged to one of the oldest tribes of Iran, and they invited us to their ceremony. A group of us traveled by bus and train and joined them for that beautiful wedding. She was brought to the party on a white horse and her long black hair was moving on her back with every movement of the horse!

When Polad had been gone for just a few months, I visited that family a few times in their very small apartment, in the heart of Tehran. The man was quiet and distant with me, but the woman was very warm and hospitable with me and the children. But one day when I knocked at their door they didn't open it!

I couldn't believe that they would actually do that, but I could see that their windows were open, so I knew they were home. When I look back I regret not having left immediately, and I still don't understand my own action of staying there in the street, constantly knocking at their door… Anyway, I got the message loud and clear! I went back home and decided not to contact any of Polad's friends any more. I thought I really didn't need to be in touch with a group of people with whom I never connected. Besides, I didn't want to be responsible for any problems they might have with the Islamic government, if I would ever be followed to their homes.

I completely lost contact with Nader, his wife and their little girl. The only people that I continued socializing with were Sepehr, his wife and their relatives in Tehran, and Polad's cousin and his family who used to live in the suburbs, my cousin, and my old friend Fafar who was married with one child.

My apartment was within ten miles of Tehran's International Airport, so during the war with Iraq we were supposed to evacuate the building. I never did! Where was I supposed to go? I had no place to go every time the air raid siren was going. It was a driving distance between Sepehr's house and my apartment, and driving was prohibited when there was an air raid on your city.

One early morning I heard something on the news about 'unsafe' air in Tehran, especially around the International Airport. I had plans to take the children to my friend's house, so I came downstairs into the street to see what was happening. There was a black film on my car, and after I looked more closely, I saw that black powdery film on everything, from the leaves on the trees to all the parked cars. I rushed back inside and decided to stay at home with the children that day. According to the news broadcasts, Iraqi war jets had attacked Tehran with chemical bombs during the early hours of that morning, so the air wasn't safe for children, the elderly and those with allergies.

I have always coughed for different reasons. Back then I didn't know why I was getting tightness in my chest and bouts of violent coughing, other than 'seasonal allergies'. Due to my problems with coughing and skin allergies I contacted The Clinic of Allergies of Tehran for an appointment. When I showed up, there were many people in the waiting room to see a doctor. One woman was trying very hard to breath and couldn't, so her face was turning red and I could see the fear in her eyes. Her husband screamed for help and after a minute or two a nurse rushed to them with an oxygen mask.

I was told that due to the chemical attack by Iraq, the number of patients with asthma had tripled in Tehran. After testing my skin for about three hundred items, they came up with a special dosage of some vaccine for me which I would receive once a week. That really helped me a lot with my cough, but not with my skin problems.

The financial freedom that I had was wonderful. I was able to help a lot of families with the extra money that I had in hand. Yes, you guessed it right, I didn't start a business and I didn't save a lot in the bank either, I spent it all! I could easily pay for the children's monthly tuition, our rent, food and gas. I spent the rest on friends who needed it. I became friends, via another friend, with an older woman who was probably twenty years older than me. This lady used to be a famous tailor in the south of Iran, and had been earning a decent living for herself and her son back in the day. After the south became a repeated target for the Iraqi war planes, a lot of families moved to other cities, especially Tehran if they had a family member there. These fugitives ran away from their homes with nothing but their birth certificates and the clothes on their backs. I helped this lady with 50000 IRR to purchase a second hand industrial sewing machine, I don't know if she ever purchased it or not!

Another friend needed money for her father's burial. As I was sitting on the floor talking to her, I put a few thousand Rials under the rug. She saw it and wanted so badly for me to take it back, but I told her that I just wanted for her mother to bury her husband without being worried about money.

However, another friend asked me to borrow 200,000 IRR to re-do her formal living room. She said that the fabric was really faded and old and she wanted to pay someone to re-do them. She received a firm "No" and was really upset and insulted, but I explained to her that re-doing her formal living room was far from emergency spending. Our relationship didn't last long after that, but I wasn't bothered by it. She was one of Polad's friend's wives.

I always went to my friends' homes with booze and food so as my presence wouldn't be a financial burden on them. As I mentioned before, we had to have government coupons for all household products including; laundry detergents, bath soaps, butter, cheese, a kg of beef (two pounds) for each person per month, eggs, milk, rice, chicken and…whatever you can think of that a family needs to live. As my mom, brother and sister were in the US, I had three extra people's share, so it was easy to be generous with food for my friends!

Now, let's talk about buying Vodka in Islamic Iran back in 1984! Firstly, I'll remind you that I have not been back to Iran for over twenty-five years, so I don't know what they do about alcoholic beverages now. I have heard that there are some places that provide these drinks for tourists, but I don't know whether it's true or not. Back then, we knew a few Armenian families in the neighborhood. They used to make homemade vodka and we would phone in advance of going to their home to pick it up! They would sell it in double plastic bags hidden inside a small size paper bag.

There were a lot of people who didn't have cars and would travel by public transport, with their purchase of vodka. Now that I think about it, what if the bag had leaked? I'm sure it must have happened to some people, and they probably abandoned the bag as if it wasn't theirs! I remember one particular family where we used to buy vodka for two years. Their house started looking better and better, and one summer they told us that they wouldn't be around for thirty days as they were going on a trip to Italy! Sepehr used to joke about them by saying:
"It's our money they are spending; they should take one of us with them to Italy!"

###

Fear August 1985

I was excited about the coming weekend: visiting day was coming up. I used to get ready for *the* day in advance. At that time I used to suffer from horrible migraine headaches too. I had a few syringes and my meds on me so I could ask someone to give me an injection in the case of sudden headache attacks. The morning arrived and I got up at 4 a.m. I knew how important it was to be one of the first people in line, and knowing the travel time would be close to two hours I had to get up early.

As I exited the apartment I locked the door behind me and I carried the children's bag of extra clothing, diapers, powdered milk, bottle and the plastic gallon of water to the car. I came back upstairs and quietly walked in to get the babies ready. Amir was sleepy and not very happy about getting up. I dressed him while he was still asleep. I had some food in the car for later when he would wake up around 7 or 8 o'clock. I wouldn't leave either of the children alone in the apartment to take the other one downstairs, and I wouldn't leave either of them alone in the car to come back up four stories to get the other one. I carried them both downstairs together. It wasn't easy, but it was the safest way.

We got in the car, Maral in her car seat and Amir on the back seat next to her. I drove towards the Azadie Square to leave the city, going towards the highway for Gohardasht. I was tired and hoping that my stomach wouldn't start one of its tricks on me where I would need to go to the bathroom when there was no way that I could find one. The babies were asleep and I was listening to some music in my car's cassette player. The road was dark and I liked it that way. People couldn't see inside the car; they couldn't see a woman with two children driving alone at that time of the day.

I passed just a few cars on the quiet road passing through, and I made good timing. We arrived through the gates around 6 a.m., and I parked the car and let the children sleep a little more. Around 6.30 I saw some movement at the main door of the building, and some people began creating a queue. I woke up Amir and after letting him relieve his bladder, gave him a cheese sandwich. Then I made up a bottle for Maral and handed it to her to drink while I was changing her diaper; she was a happy camper in no time... We were fed, clean and ready, so we slowly walked towards the small crowd. As we arrived in line, a good number of people started joining us and soon there was a long queue in front of the door.

Finally they opened the door around 7.30 and told us to enter the room one by one so they could body and bag search everybody. They let us in a large room with some folding chairs and some wooden benches. We sat down and Maral went back to sleep in my arms. Amir was a good kid and normally didn't give me a hard time by running around or walking away from me. I would have some paper and coloring pencils with me and that would keep him busy, on the floor next to my chair or bench.

Around 9 a.m. they told us to make another queue in front of a small window in that room to get our numbers. I approached the window and gave the man my husband's name, last name and his father's name. After a few minutes he said:
"Sister, your husband is not here... Next!" he called loudly.
I couldn't believe it; this was the first time that something like that had happened. Immediately, thoughts came to my mind of the families I'd seen at Evin's parking lot for their prison visits to their loved ones, and who had been told that he or she was executed...

I moved the baby on my hip and held Amir's hand firmer, bent towards the window and with a very strong voice said:
"Brother, where is my husband?"
He was already dealing with the family that had advanced to the window after me, so he wasn't happy with my interruption. I repeated my question even louder, and one of them came through the door and asked me to stand clear from the window. I moved, but kept saying "Where is my husband?" The man who had wanted me to step away told me that I had to go home and call them to find out where he was. I retorted that I had gotten up at 4 a.m. and driven for two hours, with two babies, to see my husband and I would not go anywhere without seeing him.

After a short while someone came towards us and informed us that Polad had been transferred back to Evin Prison. I dragged poor Amir out of there, jumped in my car and drove back to Tehran, towards the amusement park for Evin visitors' registration. We arrived there around 11:30 a.m. and went to a window and gave his name and information. I was told that he had been returned to Rajayee Shahr Prison (at the city of Gohardasht, Karaj) the night before!

I hastily took the children back to the car and we drove back to Gohardasht. I walked in there around 1.30 p.m. and asked for my husband's whereabouts. By this time, Amir was crying hysterically and

Maral wouldn't stay in my arms any more. The supervisor told me to take my tired and hungry children home until they could straighten out their books and see where Polad was. I screamed at him saying:
"Don't you worry about *our* kids, brother". He is crying because he wants his father; tell him where his father is!"
A few more Pasdars and mullahs walked towards me, some of them looking concerned and others shady and suspicious. They asked for my husband's full name and my home address, I had to leave while I still had control of the situation and my two children, so I walked out and very quickly drove away.

I stopped at a sandwich store in Gohardasht and we all ate and drank something before I headed towards the highway. I was exhausted, angry and frustrated. My stomach started its mean game and I regretted eating and drinking after many hours of having an empty stomach. I should have known better. I was focusing my attention on the road and trying to ignore my churning stomach, but it wasn't easy. My hands were shaking and I had cold sweat all over my body. Suddenly everything went dark... Oh my god! I screamed as I felt something on my head and face. I was frantically pulling it off my head with one hand, while driving blind with the other. It took maybe a few seconds, but I was able to pull the 'thing' off my face and head, to discover that Amir had thrown my chador (Hijab), which I kept in the car, over my head!
"What are you doing?" I screamed at him. He screamed back,
"I want Daddy!" he screamed back before hysterical crying set in... It had been such a bad day for all of us.

Finally, we arrived home and settled down. As the children took naps, I got time to sit down and have a cup of tea. Suddenly I felt like someone had hit me on my head.
"Migraine," I thought. "Okay, I have my meds and the next door neighbor can give me the shot. As my head was getting heavier and heavier on my shoulders I grabbed my meds and knocked at the neighbor's door, and luckily she was home! I was trying very hard not to throw up in front of her doorway, and as soon as she saw me she realized what was wrong.
"Do you have everything or should I bring the syringes?" she asked. I could only manage to nod my head to say yes, I had everything, and walked back towards my apartment. She immediately followed me inside and gave me the shot, and asked if I would like her to take the children to her place for a few hours. I declined and she left.

I knew, due to the injection that I had received, I would fall into a deep sleep very soon and the children would be left to their own devices. I slowly walked to the kitchen and shut down the gas tank to the stove, put all the knives inside the highest kitchen cabinet and hid the lighter and match boxes. Then I locked the front door and windows, turned on the television, and laid down on the carpet in front of the apartment door. I could hear little voices talking in the language that only Amir and Maral could understand and respond to!

I felt some soft wet things on my face and finally I opened my eyes to see my beautiful children sitting on the carpet next to me, playing like two little angels. I had a little pain around the back of my head and above my eyes, nothing harsh, but just a normal headache. I was so happy to see that the kids were doing fine and I got up and went to the bathroom. As I was passing the sink I saw my face in the mirror, Oh my God! The children had been painting my face with water colors and markers while I was out! Let's just say that I had to boil water several times that night and the day after to wash the marker pen strokes off my face!

###

Waiting and more waiting…
September 1985

Almost two years had passed since Polad's capture. The Islamic court had not yet been held, so we were waiting for the final sentence. I didn't have a phone in the apartment so I would go to the stores in my street to use their phones. They normally had a small coin box attached to the phone that would take a quarter or so to make a phone call. The problem was that they would know all about your business! After finally being able to connect with the given number, I had to fully introduce myself, and then give them Polad's full name and his father's name, before starting any conversation. It was a routine for me to try to contact the authorities once a week regarding his court status.

One day when I called from the carpentry store, they told me that Polad's sentence was seven years. I couldn't help it, I screamed:
"Seven years?!"
Everybody in the store was looking at me with sorrow. One said to another
"She should be happy he is still alive," and the other nodded his head… I just couldn't believe that he would be in jail for another seven years of his life. I was broken, and melted into a fountain of tears as I left the store in a hurry to avoid more embarrassment.

Eventually, during one of our visits, they told us that if we had a problem with the given sentence, we should go to a certain mosque on a particular date and time to talk to them. The date arrived and fortunately my father was in Iran at that time. I was able to leave the children in his care. After pulling the head cover on my head, putting on the long uniform over the long pants, I went to the address. The starting time was 7 p.m. and it was growing dark outside. I parked the car near many other cars and walked towards the building. Inside, it was as dark as a movie theater, so I carefully stepped over the entrance threshold. As I was about to move my other foot inside, I saw the face of a man lit up for a second, as he took a deep puff on his cigarette. Good thing that I saw that, otherwise I would have stepped right into him… I guess that was his plan -- for women to brush up against him as they were going inside…

"What a pig!" I thought as I edged my body away from him as I walked in. Although I hadn't bumped into him, I gagged from his smell, a mixture of nasty body odor, sweat and cigarette.

As my eyes gradually became used to the dark, I realized I was in a large room the size of a movie theater. I saw women sitting on the floor, all facing away from the entrance. I heard the sound of water and as I turned towards it I realized that the room was split down the middle by water fountains ten feet apart. Under each fountain there was a red light, so it looked like blood coming out of the fountains. They wanted to cause fear in the prisoners' families and they did a good job of that.

I sat down at the end of a row with some other women who had come with their children. Some were quiet and some were talking loudly and even joking. I still don't know if they were very brave or rather stupid. The room looked terrifying and as my eyes got used to the dark and the red light, I could see that there were at least one hundred people sitting in rows on the cold floor. Although I was a smoker, the smell of cigarettes was taking my breath away. There was no ventilation and the Pasdars and mullahs were smoking cigarettes inside the place.

Finally, a mullah asked for everyone's attention. He didn't say anything remotely useful. All he was doing was fooling the people and repeating the sickly lines about Islam, our country and how the leader Khomeini was like a father to all… Some women were telling their children to stand up and ask for their fathers. One child stood up and said: "When are you sending my father back home to us?"

The whole experience was a waste of time and I came back home having made no progress.

January 1986

It was a cold day and visiting time with Polad had finished. As I was getting ready to get to my car with the children, a young woman approached me calling out my name. I was surprised to know that she knew my name. I looked at her with a questioning face and said: "Yes?"

She seemed very young, light skinned with light brown eyes. She looked relieved and happy to have found me. Holding out a paper and a pen, she said really quickly:

"You have my furniture in your house; give me your address please,"

I hastily wrote down the address and gave it to her. We then walked away from each other, disappearing in the mass of people walking in all directions to get to their cars or buses.

A few weeks later the young woman and her brother came to my dad's house with a small truck. We had arranged it during the weekend when my tenant wouldn't be there. I opened the gate and they drove the truck inside the yard, so I could close the gate and nobody would see what we were doing. She looked at me and said:

"Wow, you look very different outside of the visiting area. You do a great job in changing your appearance…"

I had never thought of that, but hey it was a good compliment! I used my dad's key chain and opened the upstairs bedroom. That was the room where I had my mom's formal and dining room furniture stored. Here they were, this woman's clothing, boxes, chairs, wedding pictures, kitchen stuff…her whole apartment was in that room! We didn't ask each other any questions. She wanted her life back and I had it in my house. As she was getting her things loaded in the truck, I found out that she had married in a very small gathering and her husband had been captured and executed three months after they got married. I could see that she was smiling and crying at the same time when looking through her belongings…

Chapter Fifteen

The Road to Exile

Final decision, Spring of 1986

I had a financially good and mentally empty life. I had money, a home and my children. We would go to see Polad, come back home and sleep to see another day. I would drive them to the daycare at 6 a.m. and pick them up at 3 p.m. every day. I could continue to have the fun life with Sepehr and his wife like millions of Iranians who stayed in Iran and raised good children.

I, however, wasn't sure if I wanted to continue that life or not. I wasn't sure what my plans were for the future after Polad was freed from jail. I wasn't sure how I would react when Polad would start brain washing Amir, to make a freedom soldier out of him in a few years. I wasn't sure what I would do for Maral, who would be living in a closed society and always be the second class citizen in her home country. You see, I wasn't *that* Baha'i to feel powerful with my religious beliefs, to think that they would protect us. I wasn't Muslim thinking that holding my daughter back and teaching her to obey the men in her life would be the answer for her. I wasn't that politically active or knowledgeable to teach the children to be knowledgeable, but not stupid.

I knew, with or without Polad, I was about to become less in control of my own and my children's lives as the years were passing in the Islamic Republic of Iran. Still, I wasn't sure if I was ready to leave everything behind. I thought I would try to obtain a tourist visa to the US to see my family and come back to my little apartment, and make the final decision upon my return. I tried the German Embassy in Tehran. I need to explain here that all the embassies were full of applicants. People would stand in queues from the night before to get in on time and request a visa. Each country had its own rules and regulations. Iran's government had its own rules about who could and who couldn't leave the country, so it wasn't easy to get a travel visa from any embassy.

I had my and the children's translated and notarized birth certificates, my marriage certificate and Polad's legal authorization form, which I had obtained from him to visit my parents in the US. When my name was called I walked to the window and gave them my documents. The woman said:

"Happy birthday,"

"It is not my birthday until September," I replied.

"Isn't this your birth date here?" she asked.

I looked and said that it must have been a mistake. She stamped "Denied" on my request form and shouted:

"NEXT!"

I hadn't realized that women under thirty weren't allowed to leave the country. The translator had obviously done me a favor by changing my information, but hadn't told me!

A week after that, my father told me that the Swiss Embassy was giving a limited time traveling visa to approved people. That embassy was close to my dad's best friend's house, so we all drove there and I left the children with my dad to go to the embassy. I read all my translated documents first and went to the Swiss Embassy. The requirement was to have 2000 US Dollars with you, and I had that money inside my passport.

As I sat there waiting, I took out a cigarette and started smoking. Back then they didn't treat smokers like they do now, so that wasn't a problem. The problem was that I was a woman who was smoking, without being worried about the dirty looks that the other applicants were giving me. I had my legs crossed and had pushed my scarf back a little, and was thoroughly enjoying my smoke. I could see one of the embassy workers, a young woman, looking at me through the glass with curiosity.

She waved at me to go closer so I approached the window. She asked me in Farsi why I wanted to go to her country. I answered her in English, saying that I just wanted to see my family who were coming to Zurich from Pennsylvania, USA (which wasn't true). I told her that my mom and sister hadn't seen my two children, and we just wanted to see each other. She gave me a tourist visa for two weeks! I was so unbelievably excited. My dad left Iran a few days later, to come to the US, and he told my brother about the visa, so my brother sent us the plane tickets from Tehran to Zurich, Switzerland for September 1986.

I had a few months to get things in order before my "trip". I truly thought that I would be gone for a few months only. The first matter to take care of was my father's house. I contacted the tenant and told her that she needed to take her Day Care Center elsewhere. The summer was approaching and it would have been the best time for her to recommence business at a new address by the beginning of the school year. Suddenly the woman's attitude changed and that sweet talking tall woman turned into an aggressive business owner who wouldn't budge at all.

I contacted a few of Polad's friends and a gathering was arranged at one couple's house, so we could talk. Farzaneh and her husband showed up too, but we couldn't come to any agreement. My point was that I hadn't sold the house to them and as the landlord had the right to ask them to leave, and I was giving them three months to do so. Their point was that they had established a business and they didn't do all that for only two years. It was a bad situation, I was the one who had signed the rental agreement as the landlord, but we all knew I was not the sole owner of that house. I believe they were thinking of using that with the idea of never giving back the property!

Finally, during one of my visits to Polad, as I asked him to sign the 'Husband Permission Form', so I could leave the country, I also told him about the problem with the tenant. Polad listened carefully and asked for her full name. A week after that Polad's organization's attorney, the tenants and I met at another friend's house. The attorney told me that I should have known that a business wouldn't move in less than five years. My answer was to ask him to show me where I had agreed to that in our rental agreement.

Farzaneh seemed to be stressed out and began complaining that wherever she went people, relatives and friends were telling her to give the house back to me! She said:

"I don't know what you did or who you've spoken to, but everybody from all around Iran is sending me messages to move out of your property, even when our friends go to visit their family members in jail!"

I knew Polad had started that and he was doing an excellent job in spreading the word. It showed me how influential he actually was, being able to do that from his cell in Evin Prison.

The conversations took a harsh turn when Farzaneh made a face, raised her voice and said:

"I FOUND A WEAPON IN THAT HOUSE. I could do a lot of things so that you will never see this property again..."

The weapon she was talking about was the practice handgun and not real. After making that perfectly clear, I looked at her totally emotionless and calmly said:

"Have I sold you this house or have you been renting it for a year?"

She was livid and could hardly control herself. I continued:

"Look, you really don't want to do or even say this to me. Do you know why?"

"WHY?" she almost screamed.

"Why don't you ask all *those people* who have been sending you messages about giving my house back?"

Her husband knew immediately that I was referring to Polad and his connections, so he asked her to leave and talk it over at home.

Around the same time, I contacted Polad's organization and asked them for the money that they had borrowed. Within a few days the bank check was given to me for the total amount and I put it in my bank under my father and my own name immediately. The summer was right around the corner and my travel time was approaching fast. The tenant hadn't left the house while I was still in Iran.

Thinking that I would be back within a few months, I left my apartment completely furnished and with all of my belongings and drove to Tehran's International Airport with my dad and the children on a beautiful early September morning in 1986... and that was the last time I stood on Iran's soil.

Migration from Tehran– August 1986

A few friends had come to see us off. The airport was very much alive and busy. It looked like everybody was leaving town. It was loud. People were standing in line for their luggage to be carefully searched. There were probably four or five airport agents who were going through the passengers' luggage. Some were acting with real suspicion, taking out every single piece of underwear and shaking it in the air, and some were more civilized and relaxed. I whispered to the woman next to me:
"Look at that one; he seems like he is the craziest of all," and we both giggled.

I felt a presence behind me and as I turned around my eyes locked into a pair of angry eyes belonging to a Pasdar who was walking away from me.

The guy that I had pointed out as the "craziest" waved his hand towards me and said:
"YOU, COME FORWARD."

There were at least ten people ahead of me in the queue, so I knew I had been chosen to be made an example of. My dad had the sleepy children and I stepped forward with my two suit cases.
"Open them," he ordered, and I did so.
I was standing there absolutely calm. After all those years I had learned well how not to feel and therefore not to show any emotions.
"How many passengers?" he asked.
"Three," I replied.
He pointed at my fur jacket in the suitcase and said:
"Why are you taking this valuable thing with you?"
"Well, I'm going to Switzerland for the fall and as I'm sure you KNOW, it can get very cold over there!" I replied.

He asked how much gold I had with me. I had to slightly open my scarf to show him my simple and small gold earrings and then my white gold wedding band on my finger. He repeated the questions about the gold and the fur jacket two more times and I calmly answered him every time. He pointed at the two large novels I had packed and said:
"Why are you taking these heavy books with you?"

I had purchased the books for my brother-in-law who had left Iran with his family before the novels were published, and I knew he would appreciate them. So I told the man:

"I just want to keep busy reading while I'm there, so I won't be bored."

At that point he said:

"You see, we are not crazy; we're just doing our jobs as we are told."

I looked at him and said:

"I know."

They sealed the suitcase and ordered me and the children to go through the body search area. We still had some time, so I kissed my father several times and hugged him. He hugged the children and whispered in their ears that he would see them in America. I handed him my keys to the car that he had bought me five years earlier, and walked away to leave my homeland. It was very difficult to take the children and walk away from my dad and my Tehran, but I was sure that I would be back...

The children and I entered a small area where women were checking women's and children's clothing, pockets, carry-on luggage and even baby diapers. Thank God my children were no longer in diapers; they were ordering mothers to undo the babies' diapers, so they could verify that nothing was hidden inside. Their main focus was to keep the country's valuables from being taken out so they were looking for jewelry, gold and antiques. Well we all know what the former establishment had done during their shameful thirty years of ruling Iran. They sold every piece of the country's historical and valuable items to international treasure hunters.

After a humiliating body search, my children and I walked towards our gate at the airport. I can't describe my feelings at that moment. I was flying to a country where I knew no one. I hadn't lived in a free society since 1977, and had no idea what to wear or how to act so I wouldn't stand out like a sore thumb! I tried to think about being in the present moment or the next few hours, instead of trying to map out the next twenty years in my head. I had traveled by plane many times before, and had taken the children to Mashhad a year or two ago, so I convinced myself to relax for a minute.

When the plane finally took off I took off my scarf. After a few minutes the stewardess walked towards me, and bending down to my level said:

"I'm sorry madam, but as we are still in Iran's air space you need to wear your scarf."

I quietly obeyed, thinking "No problem; I'll take it off after we leave this air space," and I did!

After a few hours we landed at Zurich airport. The first few steps are normally easy at an airport as you can follow everybody else towards the main area. Holding the children's hands, I started walking towards the luggage area. That airport was huge and very busy, but quiet at the same time, so I could pull myself together and prevent myself from panicking. I saw people using luggage carts and knew I needed one. I looked around and saw them all together in a corner. I had US Dollars on me, but no coins if I needed one for a cart. To my relief, as I got closer, I saw that no coin was necessary, so I took one. There I was holding the children's hands, and struggling to push the cart too. As I was attempting to perform my 'magic act', a beautiful tall blond young woman in an airport uniform approached me saying something in Spanish. After I'd informed her that I didn't know any Spanish, she smiled and began speaking in English, telling me to follow her, as she pushed the cart to the waiting area. She asked if I was being picked up, so I told her that I needed a taxi.

I followed her to a large bright area with many counters. Escalators were running up and down, people were moving around, but there was no loud noise; it was heaven, I thought! I approached one of the counters and informed the lady that I had a reservation in such and such a hotel. My brother in Philadelphia had told me on the phone that he had made the reservation for me. She called the hotel and tried with both my maiden and married names with no luck. Somehow I had no reservation. She called around, found a hotel and called a cab for us. She specified the amount of the cab fee several times, and told me not to pay any more! She really cared about this woman with two children from the other side of the world, and that was just so amazing to me.

To keep the children occupied, and to keep Amir away from the escalator, I took them to the colorful children's area with lots of toys and coloring materials, as well as tiny toilets just for little people. I could relax a little, while the children played. After a short while the assistant at the children's area received a phone call informing her that our cab had arrived. She requested the assistance of a member of the airport staff to accompany us to where the cab was waiting. I was so grateful for the helpful staff at the airport.

I don't know anything about Zurich so I cannot tell you if I was in the good or not so good part of the city. The hotel was small with a hallway of rooms and a shower for everyone at the end of the hallway. There were two bathrooms, one downstairs where the little restaurant was located, and another one upstairs next to the shower room. Our room had two single beds, an inside wall closet and one desk. There was a window with a little balcony overlooking the street. I never opened the window.

My plan was to go to the US Embassy the next day with my passport, to get a visa for the United States. That night I tried to share a bed with both of my children, in turn, and neither of them was having that. Eventually, I put a blanket on the floor with a pillow and slept there! That was the arrangement for the entire time we were in Zurich! The next morning after cleaning and dressing the children, I took them downstairs for breakfast. Looking at the breakfast bill, I realized that we had to eat in our room from then on to make the two thousand dollars stretch far enough.

I took a cab to the US Embassy. Once we arrived there I found out that no appointment was needed. There seemed to be different areas for people based on their nationality. There were some Iranians where I was sitting and waiting to be called to the window. A young Iranian man was running around trying to help people. He asked me if I needed a translator and I told him that I didn't. I was rather perturbed when he asked where my lawyer was; this was the first time I had been told that I needed one. I really was following my nose or playing by ear!

My name was called out and I approached the window. They looked at my passport, asked some questions and stamped "DENIED" on my passport! I was baffled. My tourist visa to the US had been denied! I wanted to see my mother, sister and brother after all those years. They had never seen my children and I was hoping it could happen by us going to the US for a few weeks. I was feeling pretty devastated...

We walked back to the hotel as I had realized that I didn't have enough money to constantly take a cab to get around. I have never been good with directions, but as the taxi driver was taking us from the hotel to the embassy, I realized that the city wasn't that big, and I could find my way around on foot. As we walked back I saw a couple of stores for sandwiches, luncheon meat and fruit, so I bought a few things and took them back to the hotel for our lunch and dinner that day.

After calculating the time difference I made a call to the US, using the pay-phone in the hotel lobby. My family had to be informed that I couldn't get the US visa. Their reaction wasn't at all what I expected; I thought they were going to say that one of them would come to see us and maybe we would meet up next time...But they said:
"Stay put! You are not going back!"
I was extremely nervous, without enough money and no way to get to the US, so I thought the best secure decision was for me to go back home.

Keeping two toddlers in one small room was not easy, so to make sure the children were ready for bed, I would take them out for a walk after dinner. One evening I found a little circle within walking distance from our hotel with stores and a small movie theater. I just followed the crowd one Saturday night and found that area. It was beautiful; the train was stopped waiting for passengers, and people were walking with their families. I noticed the billboard on the outside of the movie theater; it was Sean Connery in a dark robe with a picture of a rose. I wanted so badly to go in! I hadn't been in a movie theater for almost ten years, but I wouldn't have understood the language and didn't have extra money to spend on such things.

I had to make phone calls or exchange my US dollars for Swiss Francs at the nearby bank. I would sneak out of the hotel room, and tell the girl who was washing the wooden steps or cleaning, to make sure my children didn't wander off. I would run to the bank or the phone in the lobby for no more than fifteen or twenty minutes at a time. The cleaner was pretty and very kind. She always played with the children as she was cleaning and wouldn't let them come down the stairs. She never accepted a tip from me.

One day, I decided to take the children for a little walk and we smelt the odor of burgers and some sort of beef being grilled. The children began asking for "kebab" and I really felt bad for feeding them cold cuts every day. We found ourselves in front of a Burger King and ordered a Whooper to share with the children! We sat around a round, high table. I had thought: To hell with it, I'm ordering a beer for myself too! The surface of the table wasn't really large enough and we were sharing it with a college student too. They brought my beer over and I took a sip; it didn't taste anything like the homemade beer I had had back in Iran. It was very bitter and I thought I should have ordered a soda! Before I had drunk even half of the beer, one of the children knocked it over, covering the college kid's stuff in beer! I was so embarrassed…

It must have been a week since we'd arrived in Zurich, when I received a phone call from one of my brother-in-laws who had been living in London with his girlfriend for many years. My guess was that my mother had called my oldest brother-in-law in Georgia, US and told him about my unfortunate failure with the US Embassy. He must have called his younger brother in London and given him my phone number in Switzerland.

The younger brother-in-law was a nice kid whom I remembered well from the time he was only 16 years old, and was sent to England to be saved from a rotten life in Tehran. As we were talking, he said that I should go back to Tehran and continue visiting my husband. He also told me I should be there waiting for Polad to come home to his children and take care of him with his favorite meals…. Anger welled up. Calmly I told him:

"Look, I am not his mother! I have my own children to take care of. If anybody should go to Tehran, and wait for him to come home, it's your mother and not me."

He almost screamed with sorrow:

"My poor old mother cannot go back to Iran. How would she provide for herself; where would she live?"

As he calmed down he suggested that he knew a young lady in Zurich with whom he used to be friends years ago. He said he would call her so she would come to visit us.

Claudia was the young lady who showed up at our hotel room in Zurich. What a nice, well behaved and beautiful young girl. She was maybe 22 or 23 years old, with big blue eyes and dirty blond hair, not very tall. She took us to a nice Italian restaurant one night and even got into a fender bender with another car as she was coming out of the parking space. She also gave me some of her cloths that she didn't need anymore. That was very nice of her because I had no way of purchasing clothing, to look normal outside of Iran!

My time in Switzerland was quickly coming to an end without me having any plan "B". I believe that my mother kept bothering Polad's family in Georgia, and as a result they contacted their son-in-law in Germany. This guy, who was married to one of Polad's sisters in Georgia, had been in the Persian rug business in Germany for years. They had gotten married over there years ago, had children, and as she wanted to be close to her family, they moved to the US. But he kept his business in Europe and would travel between the two countries.

Finally, three days before my visa was due to expire I received a phone call from this brother-in-law in Hamburg, Germany. He instructed me to write down an address and mail my passport to it! I was very scared; that passport was our only identity document in that country and I needed it with me all the time, but I had no other choice... I did mail my passport to that address. I have to admit that whoever that person was; they acted extremely quickly, and it was returned to me in the mail on the morning of our very last day in Zurich!

Although short, the waiting time had been torturous, but it did pass, like everything else in life passes. Our passport had the German Embassy's stamp on it. I could leave Switzerland and go to my brother-in-law's apartment in Germany. I don't remember who paid for the train tickets, but I remember it cost about 300 Swiss Francs. Claudia took us to the train station and helped me find the right train and board with two toddlers and two suit-cases. It was an overnight trip. The train was clean and beautiful like the ones you see in Hollywood movies. We had our own compartment with two sets of bunk beds. I had chosen an overnight trip so that I didn't have to cope with two youngsters wanting to run about on a moving train.

So, here I was travelling to another country after two weeks of leaving Tehran. I lay down on the seat in front of the children's bunk bed and attempted to rest. So much was going on in my life that it was making sleep escape me. There were stations on the way and you could hear a calm male voice announcing the names as the train was getting close to each one. Sometimes it would stop and sometimes it would slow down, but continue moving. The children were asleep; the compartment was small and secure; the night was wide and some lights would appear in front of the window and rapidly disappear again. Laying down in the dark and listening to the humming noise of the train was soothing me. The compartment was small enough to give me the impression of being hugged or held by strong warm and kind arms. I desperately needed that safe and embracing feeling, and was enjoying every moment of that night, imagining that everything was safe and calm in my life.

It was becoming light outside and you could see how fast the objects were flying away as the train was moving. There was a knock at our cabin door and someone checked our passport. The train started to slow down and after a few minutes came to a complete stop at Hamburg station. The children had been up for an hour or two and I was worried that 5 year old Amir would walk away from me. I gathered up all my power, took a deep breath, and concentrated on their two little hands and my handbag, as we were stepping down from the train into the crowded and noisy station.

The giant train huffed and puffed and started slowly moving, when I realized that both of our suitcases were still inside the compartment! Holding the children's hands, I started yelling and walking as quickly as I could alongside the moving train, screaming:
"My luggage, my luggage!"
The guard standing at the opening of our carriage, noticed me and I moved my arm as if I was holding a suitcase and then brought the arms up showing my palms and I moved my shoulders up as if I was saying "what happened to my suitcase?" He understood, ran inside and threw them out of the moving train one after the other! Another man who was working at the station helped me to gather them up. I had a bunch of change in my pocket from Zurich, so I gave him a handful and he was thrilled. Later on, I was told that the Swiss Franc was a very strong currency and even a few coins were very valuable.

After going through customs, we were picked up by one of the rug store employees. We were taken to the store and were soon re-united with Uncle Karim, Polad's brother-in-law. It was a beautiful large two or maybe three story store. Everybody was very welcoming and kind to us. We went to Uncle Karim's apartment at the end of the business day. He struck me as a very kind man (although he didn't really remain in his marriage later on, and caused a lot of problems for his wife and children); I will never forget his generosity and kindness to us.

The apartment was small. Most of the time, he didn't use it. He obviously had some other places to stay, so the children and I more or less had the place to ourselves. The few times that he came to his apartment to spend the night, he slept on the living room floor as we were using his bedroom! The apartment was clean, bright and warm with just a small number of pieces of light blue furniture. He bought food or would give me money. He really did look after us. During the almost ten months of our stay there, my brother was sending money sometimes, as well as Karim's kind contributions for our expenses.

As we settled in Germany I started feeling safe rather than homeless. Very soon I knew my way around and would go to the local food stores to get a few things on a daily basis. There was a small park across the street from the apartment. I would go there with the children to pass the time. Karim showed me how to use the underground train to visit his shop from time to time. We would see people and that would make an enjoyable day out. There was a television in the apartment, so we would watch television every afternoon; very soon we could all understand German!

I realized that the children needed some form of scheduling and program in their lives, so that later on they wouldn't be unhappy with school. I started to do a two hour (four thirty minute sessions) program for them every day. We would wake up, clean up and have breakfast, then sit down to sing a few children's songs together. Then we would practice English letters. I had purchased coloring pencils and markers from the nearby store and asked Karim to bring some large size blank sheets of paper. I would draw a picture of an object, for example an apple for teaching them the letter 'A'. I decided that the best method would be to present them with the English letter and the picture of the item, instead of telling them the Farsi name which they would then have to translate in their heads. We did the same thing for Farsi letters; I would draw say a picture of a horse (horse is "Asb" in Farsi) to teach them the letter 'A' in Farsi.

Then we would work on Farsi numbers for practicing math. The last portion was learning English numbers. We would have drawing class with a subject. I would say:
"Okay, let's draw 'cold' or 'angry' or 'sweet' or…" and they would draw a bunch of lines with different colors!

It was really funny and I would always tell them that their drawing was just wonderful and I could taste the "sweetness" or feel the "cold" as I was looking at them! We did great, even if I do say so myself, and when we reached the US the children were really in good shape for starting the school or pre-school classes. Doing those two hours of work helped all three of us in many ways.

Unfortunately, alcoholic beverages were very cheap and easy to get in Hamburg. I could buy a bottle of good brandy cheaper than a gallon of milk at the same store, and I started getting my brandy as I did the food shopping. Evenings were extremely lonely, especially after I was done with feeding, bathing and putting the children to bed. They would be in bed by 9 p.m. and I would be sitting watching German television while crying in my loneliness. Drinking a few glasses of wine or brandy became a nightly habit for me at that time. After waking up on the bathroom floor a few times, I realized that it was time for me to get busy with something, to feel useful and that was when we started the home schooling; I broke the descending spiral and stopped getting drunk and feeling sorry for myself every night.

One time when we took the train to visit Karim and his friends at the shop, a German man showed his extreme dislike for us and that really bothered me. Firstly, let me explain: after World War II, Germany welcomed the Turkish workers to rebuild that country. Those people worked hard and lived among Germans for decades. Many years later, some Germans began showing their dislike of sharing their country with Turks. They were questioning the fairness of Turks having the jobs, unemployment or retirement benefits, when Germans were out of work. I believe a part of this German man's angry attitude towards me and my children was because the Germans assumed that we were from Turkey. Another part was probably because young Germans just didn't seem to like foreigners, especially those who had an olive skin tone!

On that day it was really crowded on the train with no vacant seats. People were shifting and moving with the train's speed and movement, as they were holding on to the straps hanging from the roof. Nobody offered me a seat, even though I had the two little ones with me, but one seated passenger got off at the next stop. I immediately sat down, pulled Maral up on my lap and let Amir stand between my knees. In order to hold Amir's hand, I had to keep Maral sideways across my knees. Her little feet slightly touched the man sitting next to us. The man became very angry, brushing off his leg and pushing Maral's feet away, while angrily and loudly almost shouting at me. I apologized to him as soon as I noticed Maral's feet touching him and held her feet away from him, but he was very unhappy with us! The air was thick with racist attitude, which was very uncomfortable to support.

One day in the latter stages of our mini exile in Germany, the children and I left the apartment to walk to the grocery store. As we stepped on to the sidewalk a German man in his forties started talking to me. At first, he was speaking in German. I could understand some of what he was saying, but I told him I didn't know his language, and asked if he could speak English. He then said in English:
"Why are you here?"
I told him that I was waiting for my US visa and I would leave as soon as I received it. He continued:
"You have been living in this building for almost a year; you are not going anywhere. You and people like you live in my country without working and I pay for it."

I kept my cool and told him that I was a tourist and my family was providing me US dollars to spend in his damned country. I reassured him that I was not getting any government help in Germany. He began firing a deluge of nasty words at me in German, while waving his hands with agitated gestures, finally ending his speech by spitting on the ground next to my feet. I grabbed the children and hurried away, thinking that the world would never get any better, never…

There were a number of racist encounters that we had to face, but I don't want to focus on that. It was an obstacle we had to deal with on our journey, but not what this book is about. Let's look at some more cheerful and brighter episodes during our stay in Germany…

Winter came with freezing temperatures, snow and some fun events which helped us get through our 'mini exile' in Germany, as we were hanging in limbo in no man's land. Firstly, Claudia from Zurich called and told us that she was coming to visit us! We had a wonderful week together. I made some Persian meals every day some of which she enjoyed and others not. We had fun, drank some wine and laughed every day, no matter what. Polad's cousin was a college student in Hamburg at the time and he would stop by and help us sometimes. He took us with Claudia to a few places. I noticed how Claudia was looking at him! I have never known how to show a guy that I was interested, but I saw how easy it was for others when I lived in Germany!

When Claudia left I felt very lonely again, but stayed away from my nightly brandy drinking by focusing on our daily home school program. Christmas was coming; all the television programs on all three channels were about the holidays. Karim told us that he was going to the US for the holidays to see his wife and children, but some people from his store would be checking on us. Before he left for the holidays he took us to two parties in Hamburg. I will never forget them. It was like a dream come true for me to dress up and go to a real party, see people, listen and dance to some music and notice how guys were looking at me!

Karim was so thoughtful; the day before the big Christmas party he asked me if I had something nice to wear. I told him that I did, but that night he came to the apartment with a beautiful elegant gray and red tight silk dress, a pair of very expensive high heels and a long white suede coat with real fur around the neck. He had borrowed them from his partner's wife who was a beautiful German lady. I have to say that he used an excellent sense of fashion when he picked and matched them.

I looked absolutely fabulous that night! He also brought holiday clothing for the children and we all looked like royalty at that party! After the party Karim drove us around a little so we could see the Christmas lights. The whole town was enrobed in white and blue lights; it was so dreamy. I had never seen a Christmas decorated town before. As I mentioned before, I spent a few years in a Roman Catholic school and we celebrated Christmas and put decorations around the school walls, but I had never seen a whole town decorated. What a magnificent sight! It was a wonderful evening and I will always remember how great I felt that night.

###

One morning, during the spring of 1987, my brother called us from the US and told me to go to the US Embassy for my US visa. He said that he had set his alarm clock to get up at 3 a.m. US Eastern Time to make sure to call the Embassy in Germany first thing in the morning. He had spoken to someone and had explained that I was denied the US visa in Switzerland and couldn't wait another year to apply for it again. He had told them about our religion problems in Iran and the fact that I had left our homeland with two little children, and had to be able to make it into the US as soon as possible. He gave me the list of documents that I had to provide -- our passport, my lung X-ray, blood test results verifying that I didn't have any contagious diseases, our translated birth certificates and my marriage document.

We had to take a train to Frankfurt for the Embassy. Polad's cousin volunteered to take us there. Frankfurt train station was international and very crowded and huge. We arrived around 10 a.m. and took a cab to the Embassy. The plan was to show up at the appointment, get everything sorted and take the train back to Hamburg the same day. When we arrived I saw many different people from different countries standing in small groups and waiting to go inside. I saw some women with the veil and Islamic covers too, and was very glad that I was dressed very fashionably so as to let them know that I wouldn't be a problem in their country. I was wearing a mid-length leather skirt that had a long slit in the back, which Claudia had given me, with black heels and a leather jacket, which I had borrowed from Polad's cousin.

Finally, they called my name and I approached the window with Maral in my arms. The woman spoke in English asking for my documents. I gave everything to her and answered her questions. Then she asked to see the third person which was Amir. I looked around and saw Amir running like a little airplane with his arms up in the air. I tried calling him to get his attention, but it didn't work. So, I put Maral on the edge of the counter and asked the American woman behind the window to reach out and hold her; then I went to collect Amir! Picking him up and sitting him on the edge of the counter, I told him very calmly that I had been calling his name because this lady wanted to see him.
"Why didn't you pay any attention to me?" I asked.
You see, in Farsi we have the formal and informal word for "you". I always talked to the children using the formal word, so they would speak to other

people the same way. As I was done with my little speech to Amir, the woman behind the window said:

"Where in Iran are you from?"

"Tehran," I answered.

"Well, you speak Farsi in a beautiful and correct way that I've never heard anybody else do before!"

I realized that she could understand and speak Farsi and I was very happy that she liked me!

Going through the documents I'd given her, she asked for the Iranian police report. The ground was falling away beneath my feet. I had never heard of that requirement! This was so upsetting and there was nothing I could do about it. I was trying very hard to keep my tears from rolling down. She told me to come back when I had the report. As I left the building a feeling of devastation took over me; how on Earth could I obtain a Police report from Iran?

Polad's cousin was standing outside smoking a cigarette. I smoked one and told him what had happened. I was really worried. We went back to Frankfurt train station and decided to get some sandwiches before getting on the train. I was holding Amir's hand and Maral was with Polad's cousin. I saw him coming back towards me with both hands full and Maral was nowhere to be seen. Instantly panicking, I asked him:

"Where is Maral?"

"She was right here walking with me. I don't know where she is," he replied.

Calling Maral's name and still holding Amir's hand, I began a frantic search, with a feeling of sickness in my heart. It was probably about four or five minutes, but it felt like hours that I was striding in the crowd, calling my daughter's name. I noticed two very tall young men standing a few feet away from me. They looked like athletes with backpacks. They exchanged a few words and one of them disappeared into the crowd before emerging with Maral in his arms. He put her down a few feet away from me, to see if she would come to me. I took a long stride towards her, kneeled down, grabbed her by the shoulder, and with a cross between a yell and a cry told her to NEVER EVER do that again, before hugging her. Holding my crying daughter, I looked up to the young men and thanked them profusely. They both smiled and one of them bent over and tapped me on the back, saying

"No problem…"

"What a day!" I thought. We got on the train and came back to the apartment in Hamburg. I was exhausted and frustrated and seriously thinking of going back to Iran.

I called my brother the next day and told him to just let it go and not to bother with it any longer. But he contacted the Philadelphia representative and asked for help. He wrote a letter to the Rep explaining

the situation. He was told to send me to the embassy again and things would be fine this time. When he rang to tell me, I was too drained both emotionally and financially to obey, so I told him I wouldn't and hung up the phone. My dear brother would not give up on me… he got up at 3 a.m. once again to call the US Embassy in Germany and spoke to them in detail about my case. When he told them that we were Baha'i and there would be no way of obtaining a police report from Iran, they told him:
"Why didn't she say so when she was here? We would have given her the visa right away."

My brother informed them that I didn't have enough money for the second trip, so they agreed to send me the Green Card package. It took a few months, but they did send it. It was a sure thing; I was going to America and my children were finally going to see their family! After I had received the documents my brother purchased the plane tickets for us from Hamburg to JFK airport for during September of 1987.

Life was changing for me and the children. I was anxious and exited yet trying to carry on the daily life and keep the children busy with our morning classes. I was really lonely and needed so badly to have a conversation with an adult for a change! One day, there was a knock at the apartment door and as I opened it I saw a young woman in her late twenties, smiling at me. She said that she wanted to talk to me about Jesus for a few minutes if I had some time for her. Time was all that I had and I desperately needed to talk to someone, so I smiled and eagerly invited her in!

She was a Jehovah's Witness. I just wanted to see another person so I just sat, politely letting her talk to me. The second time she came, she brought another lady along with her who was a little older; we had a pleasant hour together and they left. I bought cookies and orange juice and waited for them to come over! Well, that's being really lonely, when you count the days for a religious group to come and talk to you! Due to my Catholic school background and also Baha'i school I was very familiar with Christianity, but their point of view was different. They didn't care for wearing a cross necklace, for instance. They made sense with that one:
"If someone that you loved was killed by a gun, would you wear a gun around your neck as a necklace?" she asked.

I was enjoying their company until they started wanting more of me; they wanted me to show my support and join them at some meetings. It was time to tell them the truth, that I really didn't care much about their religious views and just enjoyed their company. I don't think they ever believed me and they continued to come over and talk to me. They even asked me about my origins and brought some books in Farsi about their beliefs!

The day finally arrived and Karim took us to the airport in a cab. I was dressed in my best clothing. I had rolled my hair the night before and made it look really pretty. The children were dressed smartly too. He dropped us off, helped with giving in the suitcase at the luggage counter and left. He told me that he would see us in America soon. When the children and I approached the airline check-in desk they asked us to enter a room and wait. I don't know what that was all about. They looked at my passport which didn't have a US stamp on it, but I had the dossier that was sent to me from the US Embassy.

I think they had to make sure of something or perhaps they searched our luggage during that time, but we sat there for a good hour until they finally told me that we could board the plane...

I really have no words to explain how I was feeling on the way to New York. I think the best way of putting it would be to say, I didn't believe that it was real. I kept telling myself that I could do all my dancing for joy when I actually arrived there. It has always been my way of dealing with potential good news to minimize my disappointments if things went wrong. I try to control my feelings in case something unexpected may arise. I quietly and calmly walked to the plane holding my children's tiny hands...

We did land in what was to be our new homeland. We had made it! As we disembarked, the pilot and the flight attendants all said goodbye to me in Spanish! I don't know Spanish at all; perhaps I should learn.

JFK Airport was so crowded and so loud. It was with glad relief that I could read all the signs in English. I found the way quite easily and we were soon standing in a queue for those possessing a Green Card dossier. When it was my turn I handed the folder to a man, sitting on a folding chair, behind a simple folding table. After opening the folder he took some sheets out, handed me back the remaining sheets, and stamped my passport. He then pronounced the magical formula:
"Welcome to America."
At that moment I knew that it was for real and those three words from that stranger's mouth were the most beautiful words I had heard in a very long time.

We walked out of the gate and I saw my brother on the other side of the railing, looking searchingly at the crowd. I called his name and waved at him numerous times, but he was looking through me, without recognizing his sister after ten years. Finally, I managed to get nearer to him. After calling his name again, he turned towards me and exclaimed:

"Ah...it is you then..."

He hugged and kissed us in turn. He continued talking as we were walking towards the luggage area. He explained:

"I was standing there wondering who this Spanish woman with two kids waving at me was!" Amir was sleepy and Maral was holding my brother's hand and jabbering non-stop in a combination of German and Farsi! My brother was just nodding his head in agreement and telling her, "Yes, you are right; aha, I understand." Later on he told me he had no idea what this little bird was saying to him that night!

Arriving at the luggage area we saw my father waiting for us. That was great; the children bloomed in a moment when they saw grandpa who they knew from Iran. It was one year after we had left Tehran. We entered the United States of America on September 21st 1987, one day before my 31st birthday... I could now allow myself to dance for joy!

Chapter Sixteen

New Beginning

USA 1987

After hugging and kissing each other we got into my brother's car, so he could drive us all to Pennsylvania where our new home was waiting for us. As soon as we sat in the car my brother handed me a piece of paper with directions and told me to read it to him as he was driving! I had just arrived there; yes I knew the English language like everybody else who learns a foreign language in school. No, I didn't know the abbreviations such as "N" for North and EX for exit…so after ten minutes I said left and then I realized that it should have been right and it was too late… The bottom of my poor brother's car hit the island in the road while he was at full speed and he had to call for a tow truck…

My brother had to walk from the damaged car to one of those highway emergency phones to make the call. The truck arrived and the driver agreed to let us in the front as he was towing the car to New York. The back window of his truck was open and the cold wind was coming in directly towards my head. I was so embarrassed with the situation that I didn't say anything during that awful ride. I remember there was my dad, me and the children in that truck, but cannot remember where my brother was; maybe he was sitting in his car…I don't know!

In any case, the truck driver dropped us off at the train station in New York around midnight. I had two heavy suitcases, two little children and my old father with me. To make matters worse, I was wearing a tight skirt and damn high heeled shoes too!! I told my dad to hold the children's hands and let me be worried about the suitcases. It must have been one funny scene, with me taking a deep breath, picking up two suitcases, making a face and walking a few steps and putting them down, again taking a deep breath, making a face and…. There were two guys standing at the corner talking. One of them said to the other: "Ten bucks that she'll take four steps this time and not five"!

We finally made it into the station. Oh my God what a busy train station it was! Although my father wasn't that good at speaking English, he knew well where to go and what to do. With his help we all got into a train for Philadelphia. After about maybe two hours or so we arrived at the station in Philadelphia; we had successfully made the trip and were waiting for my sister to come with her car and pick us up.

I was sitting on a bench with sleeping Amir's head resting on my arm and talkative Maral standing close to my knees. My brother must have called home and told my sister about the car accident and change of plans. As physically and emotionally exhausted as I was, I still didn't miss seeing my sister walking towards us through the crowd. She was tall with beautiful dark and long wavy hair framing her beautiful face and wide smile. She had black leggings on with a black and white designed long sweater. She took a few long steps and we hugged and kissed after ten years of separation.

My sister grabbed a suitcase and I took another as we made our way to the car. I was thinking that I had seen my father, my brother and sister and I couldn't wait to see my mom after all those years.
"Wow, she is going to see her only grand-children for the first time!" I thought to myself and was excited at the thought.

New "Home"

I had finally reached the US and my family. Was it to be a joy ride from thereon in? Far from it... There were still battles to be breached. I don't actually have a detailed memory of those early hours or even days. But I do know that I had mixed feelings and was in denial. All the signs were there...yes, telling me that I'd left Iran, my apartment, with all I could carry – my two precious children – and I'd come to the US to start a new life. However, deep inside, for some reason, I kept thinking and telling myself that I'd be going back. When I left Iran I hadn't cut my emotional ties – I didn't say "Goodbye". I had left thinking that I was escaping for a couple of months and then I'd go back.

Did I do that knowingly? Was I lying to myself or was I tricked by family into permanently coming out of Iran? I can't tell you. I left the apartment, picking just a few items to bring with me. I can still picture my hair brush next to the mirror and a pair of shoes, I'd put on the top shelf in the closet because it wasn't the season for wearing them... The chairs, the rug, the curtains, the fridge, the stove, the red table in the kitchen where I fed the babies...are all still in place in the apartment in my mind. So, I really did have a feeling that I'd go back, deeply embedded in my subconscious. I guess my ego felt safe with the idea that I could go back and everything would be familiar again. The ego doesn't like change, and I suppose that is how I can put together me being in the US for a new life, starting over again, and still thinking that I would be returning to Iran. My ego was reassuring me and keeping me safe, as only it knows how. The ego isn't past lying to us, if it thinks it is keeping us safe!

It was a strange situation for me. I'd come to live in a household with my younger sister who'd just graduated from college, a brother who had become the head of the household, and a mother who had come down some notches in class from what she had been accustomed to in Iran. She used to be a teacher who worked part-time to have some money of her own, and be able to go the hairdresser, have fine jewelry, a maid and a gardener. Now she was a woman wearing jeans, working odd jobs and at a hairdresser's. Mom had become qualified to work in the hairdresser's, which is rather amusing when I can remember that thirty years before a hairdresser would not have been at her level to talk to!

I remained in denial for some time... Then I saw how my children could flourish here, and I told myself:
"Okay, I can stay here until the kids have had an education and can stand on their own two feet...maybe when they start college, I'll go back..."
I was riddled with homesickness, but then I had been homesick even when I was still in Iran, because the revolution had resulted in everything being taken away. It had all changed – listening to music, being carefree and walking in the streets, talking to people, laughing, going to the movies, and riding a bike... Yes, all had changed and I was hopelessly homesick while still in Iran. But while I was there, there were still physical things around me, to look at and be a kind of band-aid for me. When I left, there was nothing of my former life and I missed everything.

I missed walking down the street, around the corner, the flowers coming down from the yard, hanging into the street, from above. I can still smell the scent from those flowers. For decades I'd walked on the street, ever since I was allowed to walk outside on my own, from 9 years old until I married Polad, and then afterwards, when I went back to the family home for the short period, with my children. Memories of going to school, walking with friends and laughing out loud, the corner store, early school years...I missed everything. Loneliness was my partner at that time.

I certainly did not feel total relief once I'd arrived in the US. Remember, when I came here, I'd been living on my own for a number of years and was habituated to that. I had been the head of my own household. I'd got married when I was very young; my husband had been taken away; I had been the person who ruled my life and that of my children. Now, I had come, with my two children, to someone else's house and was supposed to be the house guest falling in line with the homeowner's rules and habits. It was polite on my part to be how they wanted me to be, not to make waves, not to come up with ideas about what they were doing right or wrong, not to suggest what could be improved upon, or anything.

It was extremely difficult for me and the family didn't understand how I was feeling. Mom was playing the role of the mother in the house, and my sister, in her late twenties, was the baby in the family structure, while my brother was playing the role of a father. Everything was done towards satisfying the baby sister – her sleep, her work, her school – and I was just an extra package, along with my children. No matter how much I tried to keep this package quiet, colorless or invisible, it wasn't easy.

Amir had grown up in Tehran, asking me every day why other children had a family. Other children would talk about their aunts and uncles, cousins and grandparents…
"How come we don't have anyone? We only have Grandpa and he comes and goes…"
All the time while we were in No Man's Land in Europe, I occupied him with the thought of soon being reunited with his family. Then we eventually arrived in the US and everything was hunky-dory for the first few days…and then everything changed. The situation gradually became rather fraught.

They wanted to discipline my children; they wanted to feed them how they thought best… I was their mother and chief; I was the one who had taken them across the world. I had given birth to them, and I knew them better than anyone. My family hadn't had young children around for over twenty years. I came along with the children and was seen as one of the children myself. They hadn't witnessed the process of me becoming a mother. It wasn't easy for my mother to adapt to the idea of me being the mother, the chief, the person who had the right to say yes or no to the children. There was almost a difficult element of competition.

Mom, for instance, had her habitual television shows – the soap operas would start at about 1 p.m. I wanted the children to watch the cartoons to help with their English learning. The cartoons would start at about 4 p.m. as the soap operas were ending. Grandma would turn off the television at that time, telling Amir that the television had been on for hours, and should be turned off to give the tube inside a rest, so that it didn't burn out. It would have to be kept off for an hour – cartoon hour. I considered that selfish and not a very kind gesture!

After a couple of months, Polad's family in Georgia wanted to see me and the children. A relative drove the eight or nine hour journey, stayed the night with us, in my brother's house, and the next morning drove us to the family in Atlanta. They really wanted me to stay with them in Atlanta, which I could understand…I was a young woman and they wanted to make sure I wouldn't start dating. They wanted the children to be with their family and cousins, but after about two months I realized that I couldn't stay there – the other children were beating up my children. Their way of raising children was so different to mine; it was very American, letting the children do whatever they wanted. They thought I was too strict with the children and not allowing them to be go-getters. I wasn't comfortable with their attitude.

While we were there, I'd expressed my concern over the television problem with my mom. So, once we had returned to my brother's house, a television arrived from Polad's mother. I appreciated that very much. It was a great help in appeasing the situation with Mom; the children could watch the television for a few hours. However, my brother developed concerns over two televisions on at once and two sets of lights, increasing the electricity bill... He would politely come to invite us to watch television with Mom, in the one room. Back to square one!

My brother had bought this beautiful house in Philadelphia years ago when he was a college student. We never discussed money while I was living at home with my parents, so I'm not sure how the money for purchasing that house came about. I remember hearing from my mother that my brother "saved" the down payment through his daily lunch money and hard work. On the other hand, I knew that my parents were sending him money every month for him to live in the US. As soon as the revolution took place the price of the US Dollar started going up; therefore the monthly funds must have been shrinking. I think the combination of some money from Iran and his hard work and savings paid for that house.

When I saw the house it seemed really large to me. There were two doors, one in front of the building, which opened into the formal living room with the stairs for the second floor, and one on the side via the driveway, which opened directly into the large den with its soft fluffy wall to wall carpeting and wide windows overlooking the green and lush yard. You could enter the kitchen, which was in front of the den from either door.

Before the children and I arrived, the family used to sit around in the den watching television together and entertaining friends. There were three bedrooms upstairs, one for each person, and a shower / bathroom. My family gave us the beautiful large den to live in. We had three single beds and our own bathroom behind the kitchen.

My uncle's American wife, Helen helped me with enrolling the children in pre-school and First Grade. She walked me through everything including getting the vaccination reports for the children for the school district. It was all so foreign to me; I didn't know where to go or what to ask... She was an angel and put her life on hold for weeks to help me and I always think of her with love and respect.

My mother, sister and brother were all working. My brother was an Electrical Engineer, but had had a hard time finding a job and was working somewhere absolutory unrelated to his education just to bring in some money. I think my sister had just graduated from college with an Engineering degree as well and had just found a job. To my surprise my mom, who used to have maids back in Tehran, was working odd jobs such as being a hair dresser or even as a packing person in a candy and chewing gum factory. They seemed to be happy, tightly knitted together and always busy. They had a fast paced life and here I was with no car and no job, staying at home every day after they would all go off on their daily schedule.

During those first weeks I used to try to keep busy by cleaning a bathroom or vacuuming the rooms, just to be helpful. As much as I was trying so hard to not cause any changes in my family's routine, I had made huge changes by just arriving there with two children. They were trying so very hard to make us feel at home. They were kind, but not very thoughtful. I believe one of the problems was that they had no bonds with my children. They weren't present when I became a mother for the first and then second time. They weren't there when my belly was growing and a new human being was forming within my body. So no matter how hard they were trying to get close to me and my children, I could feel the distance and that bothered me more than I care to talk about here.

I had initially thought my mother would grow a pair of wings due to having her grandchildren around, but she didn't respond to my children that way. My family was going through some financial hardship, and having me and my children couldn't have been easy for them. I had everything that I needed within their home -- food, clothing love and a nice room. I knew well not to over step the boundaries with my mother. I had been the woman in charge of my own home for many years by then, and knew to not even try to cause any problem for my mother's role in that house. I never cooked in her kitchen because of that reason.

I am sure that I was the other side of that problem too. I had changed a lot during my marriage to Polad and living through a revolution, enemy attack on my country (Iraq and Iran war) and a civil war. It was as if, for ten years, I had constantly been walking one way, and they had been walking in the opposite direction. Thus, the valley between us was huge. Although I had lived an emotionally hard life, I had still retained some of my snobbish paradigms from my childhood. On the other hand, my family in the US had had to start from zero in many ways, to survive the immigration, and that had made them even more different from how they had all been back in Iran.

My mother who had always had help at home in Tehran, was now working as a hairdresser in the US and would dress in jeans, which was a complete culture shock for me! My sister was an engineering student who looked and acted like a normal college kid. What I wasn't there to see was that she had had to go through hell to pay for her college tuition. I remember one silly case that bothered me when I had just arrived there. The spoons and forks in the house were extremely light weight and small! I know it sounds really stupid, but it took me weeks to get used to eating with those cheap utensils... Ah, if I only knew what they had been through to even have a normal life in the US.

After a few short months I had the use of a car. Mom had always wanted to drive and she couldn't. She had learned how to drive back in Tehran when she was in her fifties. As is often the case with people who learn to drive later on in life, she wasn't a good driver. She had a car sitting there, not in use. So, I asked her if I could use it for little things here and there, and she agreed. Soon after that I was able to find a part time job in a woman's clothing store. The pay was very little ($4.75 per hour), but it took me out of the house.

My mother came through and helped me to sign up in a local community college and take some courses, thanks to a grant. However, this brought up an issue between us. Mom wasn't happy watching me driving off in her car every morning. I would see her standing at the bedroom window watching. The poor woman was jealous, and even claimed that I was mistreating her car. As a positive outcome, my sister and her fiancé at the time found me another second hand car. Mom must have paid for it.

By going to school and working, I wasn't home that much and when I came home I didn't appreciate the way my children were being treated. It wasn't that they were torturing them, but I couldn't tolerate anybody, apart from me, punishing them. I even talked to a psychologist and brought the information home to my mother and sister. I explained to them that as I was told by the doctor, there should only be one disciplinary person in a child's life and not the whole family, but nobody would listen to me. It was a somewhat frustrating situation to work through.

I would come home from my part-time job or community school classes to find my children unhappy, which then saddened me. It gradually became clear that Mom was trying to play the part of their mother, and she was treating my little girl very harshly. There was a history of this in my family, which had actually been apparent to me since my childhood. My mother and a great deal of other family members had a problem with girls. They obviously preferred the male variety. This was very evident now, with my children. Mom wasn't treating my daughter and son on an equal basis. She was even of the opinion that I was mistreating my son because he resembled his father! As grateful as I was for being in the freer system of the US, I couldn't wait to get the hell out of there!

Eventually my brother, who had originally purchased that house sold it and divided the profit equally among the four of us, which was a very generous gesture on his part. With the $20,000 I was able to make a down payment on a house and move away to live my life and raise my children on my own. I still have that house where I brought up my children. It became a true home for us.

Our new home

At that time, I was a nobody in the US and I had no credit status, so my brother co-signed with me. I have to say, I didn't let him down. The mortgage was paid every month without fail. I had been given the opportunity to have an office job, with my sister's help, in the company where she had just started working as an engineer. The monthly mortgage was around $900, and then, of course, there were other expenses such as utilities, food and clothing. No matter how much I tried putting plastic on the windows and to cover the air conditioning ducts, the little house had a high electricity and gas bill, for some reason that escapes me.

It wasn't at all easy for me and most of those early years I worked two or even three jobs at once to pay the bills. My jobs were a combination of office work from 8 to 5, waitressing and/or fortune telling in a bar from 8 to midnight, deli worker and one year of being a gas station attendant. I became very familiar with consignment shops for my clothing and furniture for our house.

Memories of those years in the US are another interesting subject to write about at another time. But I will recount a few, to give a better picture of my experience and situation...

When I moved to my little house, I gradually reduced connections with my family, gaining my space, my freedom, my life. It seemed as if my brother felt that as he had co-signed, to help me have the possibility of buying my home, he could come and go as he pleased. I found his shaving and toiletry items in the downstairs shower, and I wasn't at all comfortable with that. It was an intrusion. I had been waiting for so long to be head of my little abode, and have my privacy, and raise my children as I saw fit. It didn't go down well with him, when I rang him to request that he remove his things, but I wanted to freely establish my family life with my children.

That wasn't easy with my family's attitude. A basket of fruit was delivered by a family member, along with instructions to share the fruit with my sister, brother and mother. In an effort to find out what the deal was with my new home, I rang my sister to find out what I hadn't been told. I learned that they had decided that my house, which was in the same area as their old house, would become the center for our family to get together. They wanted to keep the relationship they had grown between them, while all living together, and have a free pass to come and go as they wished. That was a "No" for me.

People would call for my brother and I would tell them that there was no such person living in the house. I stopped answering the phone. There was a big falling out between my mother and I over her interference with my parenting methods, which resulted in my mother being banned from my house and her not seeing her grandchildren for five years, which was a great shame.

It was all too much for me. Thus, as far as I was concerned, the price I was expected to pay for what my family had given me was too high. Maybe I was being a bit ungrateful, but it wasn't my house yet, with all this going on. I needed to lead my life, with my rules, my children and me in control, paying the bills and taking full responsibility. I needed them to respect my boundaries, and let me be independent.

In order for that to happen, I had to find two more jobs because with my income and the mortgage it was impossible to make ends meet. I found a waitressing job at a diner. So, I would do a forty-five minute drive in the morning to my day job. The children would be in school, across the street from our house. At 5 p.m. I would come home, driving like a maniac, to get back at about 5.45, to collect the children from the after school program – or they would walk across the street with the road crossing patrol person. They wore a door key round their necks.

After feeding them, checking their homework and bathing them, I would leave to go to work in the diner at 8 p.m. until about Midnight. Sometimes I would have $10 or $15 in tips in my pocket and I could go food shopping in the twenty-four hour food store. After Midnight fruit and fresh produce was cheaper, because they reloaded the shelves at about 5 a.m.

Even with the diner job, I still didn't have enough money coming in to pay the bills, so I found a third job in a bar/restaurant. One of my girlfriend's Russian mother had taught me how to read a deck of cards as a game. I told the restaurant staff that I'd like to read the cards for their clients at $10 a go. They tested me; I had to read the cards for the waitresses and the manager, so that they could see. Some were impressed; others told me to stick to my day job, as I wasn't even close! Well, I got the job, and I didn't have to give commission to the restaurant. They didn't have to pay me any money for being there either. I would go there at weekends, all evening until the restaurant closed at about 2 a.m.

It was rather hit and miss. Sometimes I would sit there alone in a bar, away from my children, and wouldn't have any customers. Other times, I might earn $20 for my efforts. Sometimes I would get weird customers. I was a 31 year old attractive woman sitting with a deck of cards in front of me. There were many drunks who thought I was there for something else! One night, there was a very distraught lady sitting at the bar with her husband. She agreed to me doing a reading for her, but became very upset as I began the reading, yelling and screaming at me that I wasn't anywhere close. Apparently, their son had been involved in a car accident and was in a coma; they were visiting to find out if he was going to make it or not…

After returning her $10, I tried explaining to her that there isn't really anything in the cards; it involved a connection between the client's brain and my brain. The client has to be open to connecting, sending and receiving the energy. If that isn't the case then I can't receive the energy and decrypt it. So, it's actually an act of thought-reading rather than card-reading. This made her even angrier, calling me a charlatan and con-artist. I had to distance myself from her and cut my losses.

My sister heard about me doing the card readings. She had bought a house about half an hour away and would visit. She began reading cards at the same establishment. Her English was much better than mine and her readings were so good, which resulted in her taking my place at the restaurant. I was no longer required. That was the end of that.

This all illustrates the struggle in my life. For the first time, I had to go to second-hand stores to buy suits to wear to my new clerical job, which my sister had found me. There we were, side by side dressed in suits… This probably bothered her because she knew that I had no money. To rub salt into the wound, thanks to the pressure and sadness in my life, I was looking great figure-wise, having dropped down to size 4. My sister admitted to me that she was bothered by my small frame. Sisterly rivalry is a strange thing. There was I, unable to buy lunch and hardly managing to pay for the gas to drive to work, and here she was, bothered by my look in my second-hand suits!

Despite this being a rather difficult period for me, I began to feel good about myself, especially when I began writing checks to pay the bills. I felt a sense of being in control. It felt so comfortable to be able to walk around the house in my nightie, to lock the doors, pull down the shades and have my little house protecting me… Yes, I felt good about myself – it was almost the same feeling as when I lived in my father's house in Tehran, when I was growing up. It was reminiscent of having my own room, with its desk, phone, little radio, kerosene heater, tea or hot chocolate – my little sanctuary. I had found my little sanctuary again. It may have been costing me a lot, in various senses, but my goodness, the feeling was unbelievable, indescribable.

A lot of the traditions I'd grown up with during those years in my father's house stayed with me. I transferred the beliefs about the relationship between parents and children, for example, on to my children. There was a religious side to such traditions which I "rephrased" to suit our family. Although I had been brought up as Baha'i, and I put my children through Baha'i school, I didn't force them to pray or fast or such things, but the core of what I was brought up in was transferred to my children.

One of the core issues was you do not lie. If what you did is so bad that you have to lie about it, why did you do it? If it wasn't bad, then why do you have to lie about it? Another important issue was that of touching or taking something that doesn't belong to you. I realized that many families didn't have the same outlook. So many children seem to take whatever they see and think that's acceptable behavior. If it belongs to Mom they seem to think that's okay… if it belongs to Dad they seem to think it's theirs. This is something I was very pushy about. You should know your rights and separate everyone else's property from your own.

I eventually came up with a list of house rules (and I still have them). I would type it up at work and stick stickers around it, and frame it and put it up on the wall. For example:- If we are out of the house for more than two hours we have to call or check in. Don't go anywhere after school without Mom knowing… (I would write "without the other ones knowing" because I would follow the same rules). Don't invite anyone indoors without talking about it in advance. We're a complete family and we don't need another member to make our family complete. (I put that there because I didn't want my children to feel that because there wasn't a father in the house our family wasn't complete. For your amusement, I've put a list of house rules as an appendix…

Little by little, my finances improved enough for me to be able to request that my brother pull out of the co-ownership of the house. His name was taken off the title deed and I was free and independent. I felt so good about myself that I could start dating. I will point out that I was no longer married… Let's backtrack to the final months when I was still living in my brother's house, for a brief explanation…

The telephone call

Back in 1991 I received a phone call from Polad in Iran. He was released from prison and wanted us to go back and be a family with him. He thought we needed to give our marriage another try. My thoughts didn't coincide with his! I was already in the process of buying my little house, and no longer had any intention of returning to Tehran.

I can recall the phone conversation very well, in which I told him that our marriage was a mistake. He asked why I was saying such a thing. "We were in love," he added.
"No, it wasn't love. It was habit. We were just used to being together."
"But I loved you, Azita…"
"I don't think I loved you…"
"You didn't love me?" he asked.
"In the beginning, when we were girl and boy-friend, I loved you…but at the time when we were married, I didn't love you in that way anymore," I answered.
"Not even when you gave birth to Amir? You didn't even love me then?"
"No. I loved Amir, but I didn't love you."

It was true...I wasn't happy even during the good days of our lives together. He was having a very hard time digesting what I was telling him, and the conversation gradually became tenser, as he wanted to have the children back in Iran.

"You know I'm not going to allow my children to grow up in that country..."

"You do what you have to do... They will grow up here, and if you cause any problems, I'll go to the authorities and make it extremely difficult for you to ever come here."

"Well, congrats on your new house, country and life. We'll see how that goes..."

End of conversation...

Cutting the ties...

Immediately after that phone call I filed for divorce. I hadn't done it while he was in prison as I hadn't wanted to cut off his hope that someone was out there waiting for him. Now I had to completely and definitely cut the ties, because if our marriage continued and he turned up in the US he could cause trouble for me. I contacted my uncle who had been in the US for fifty years or so, and he put me in touch with a very good friend who was a lawyer. As there was no property sharing involved, (we had nothing together and I wanted nothing from him – I just wanted to be divorced from him), everything went through within six months or so.

Thus, the divorce was happening at the same time as we traversed moving into our new home, and moving out of my brother's house, with the shaky ties and emotion that involved with my family. Stressful period indeed!

Happily it didn't last. Life began smiling at me. I settled in my new terraced home, and after some months I began dating. This proved to be hard-going...I had never dated before. This was the all new experience that was totally alien to me. I really didn't know how to comport myself, as I mentioned earlier in the book. There were some disasters, I have to admit. Some men took advantage of me, never called back and didn't become emotionally involved; that is, until I became more "streetwise" on the dating front and began having proper relationships. I kept my dates well out of my children's life. Instinct told me that the children shouldn't be exposed to these relationships.

Oh dear, I got it completely wrong one time, and I still apologize to my children for that one! One man was revealed to be an alcoholic. He actually moved into our house, as a tenant in the basement, before I realized. That really didn't work out well at all... One alcoholic kicked out!

My ex-husband did show up in our lives some years later. I think he hadn't been authorized to leave Iran for five or seven years after being in jail. He finally popped up in a southern state of United States, and had remarried. I received a lawyer's letter informing me that Polad was seeking full custody of the children. Amir was now about 12 years old and Maral was 10. I had to contact the same lawyer who had helped me with the divorce.

An appointment was scheduled at court, and we respected the appointment. Amir was shaking, quivering, and crying.

"My father has no right to come into my life and leave as he wishes. He can't do this to me," he sobbed. He began remembering vague memories of when he was very little and his father was still at home with us. But he was very young, as you know, when Polad was taken away. Although I wanted to win the battle, I couldn't tell the children that it was their father's fault.

"I don't like him, and he didn't treat me well, but it wasn't his fault. They took him away," I felt inclined to tell them. But deep in the depths of my mind there was a thought lurking:- It was his choice. He had gambled with us and he had lost us. Maybe, the children had absorbed and taken on some of those thoughts lurking in the depths of my mind.

The meetings were a painful struggle. Here I was, battling for my little family's well-being, yet again. When would my life transmute out of density into grace and ease? Did I deserve this? When was I going to come out on the sunny side of life, smiling, safe and secure with my precious children?

To put it bluntly, the moves thrown out by the opposition in the wrestling ring were lies! Drawings were produced by some young children (from his family, I presume). Supposedly, my children had been in contact with their father, sending him pictures they'd drawn. Seriously? That was funny!

"You mean these two young children have gone to the post office and mailed these drawings?"

If anything like that had taken place it would have been me going to the post office, and that had not happened.

My lawyer was married to a very nice Iranian man. She was sympathizing with Polad and the potential father and son relationship. She asked me in many ways and words to calm down and allow Polad access to the children and be a part of their lives. Well, I did mellow and although I retained custody of the children, it was eventually agreed that Polad would also have rights as far as access was concerned.

The process began with child support. I don't know how much he was earning, but his wife was an architect. They proposed two hundred dollars per month for the child support. My shopping cart for a week was more than one hundred dollars! Little by little, I mellowed and allowed him half day visits. As the children were growing older, I allowed them to visit him in south for two week periods. He would pay for the flights.

He wouldn't help me with big expenses for the children such as the dental specialist's bill of thousands of dollars, but he'd hire a boat to take the children out on an ocean trip. Polad was the dad who would give them everything they wanted...even cars when they were old enough. Despite my sarcasm, I have to say that I couldn't buy my teenage son and daughter a car. He could and I am grateful that my children were blessed with these presents.

Polad became who he wanted to be, but he had missed much of their childhood years, and he would never be able to get that time back. So I didn't say anything. We avoid talking to each other these days...even after all these years our relationship is volatile and an argument can very easily erupt.

Everybody has been happy with the arrangements over the years. I was able to do well for my children between 1989 and 2004 and they both became well educated, kind and responsible people. I met my current husband back in 1999 while we were both working in the same company. He was a single dad and I was a single mom, so we understood each other very well as kindred spirits. He was a huge emotional and financial support for me during those years when I was just programmed to make life good for my children. He reminded me that I was a person who deserved love and happiness too. He has been my rock in life ever since I met him. We met and fell in love, but didn't get married until my children had gone through college. We have been married for a few years now and I have the love and harmony that I had always been yearning for. ..

Epilogue and Legacy

Feelings, fears and sudden numbness will always remain with me.

I believe that my life has been an extraordinary one. To be honest, some times when I look back it surprises me to see how I made it through. There was a big difference between my childhood and lifestyle at that time and what I went through from the time of my marriage onwards. It's a mystery to me how I got through. Being a middle child did make me independent; I learned from a very young age not to count on anyone else, for anything. That was no doubt a major reason why I didn't break. I had the habit of relying on myself and my own capabilities, which I drew on from deep within. The hero came along with the strength to see and grab the opportunities for going forward, when they arose.

Even when I was married, I didn't count on Polad. He thought he was the protector, but I would strongly argue against that. Having said that, he was protecting me by not giving me information about his organization and activities. Later on, when I was interrogated, I had no information to render. That protection is something that I was grateful for, and is something that I will not forget.

As I stated in the prologue, I originally started writing my memoir as a form of therapy to help myself in remembering those strange days of my life, and get over my anger towards life in general! After a while I felt that I needed to let my children and their future children understand where we came from and why we left our homeland to live and raise our families in another country. I needed to share my strength with those who scream "Life is not fair" when facing the smallest obstacles in their lives. What I wanted to share is about the moment that I found myself with no job, no family and no money, with two small children and a husband who was missing, up to the stage of my journey where I came through; that is, I raised two wonderful people and am now living a contented life. I wanted to share the lessons I learned from that journey.

I still see the world like a war zone and that has affected me a lot in dealing with people....everybody is an enemy until proven wrong...every situation is survival and not living. Every fight is a war and not an argument to solve a problem. This memoire is Azita standing up for love and justice.

I hope you realize, after reading this book, that Iran is not a country of fundamentalists. How you see it in the West is not the true Iran. The revolution took place because different groups of Iranians were not satisfied with the situation in their country, but their dreams were crushed by the new fundamentalist regime. I'm sure there are many more who, like me, believe in women's rights, human rights and a liberal education. Like me, many can see that the religious fundamentalism is hindering the development of Iran and repressing its people. Not only does it take away the material things that people enjoy, but it takes away their dignity and even their identity. That cannot be right.

This book is drawn from my heart and is the evidence of two revolutions which touched me deep to the core. My identity, my "being" was revolting. Thus, there were two revolutions – my own and that of my country…

The Lost Generation

Now we've come to the end of this phase in the story, you may be wondering what happened to some of the characters…

Mom's ending

Mom developed her own numbness, living alone in the US, and descending into the abyss that is Alzheimer's disease. It became almost impossible to leave her alone when she was around 77, what with her hallucinations, forgetting to eat and often wandering the streets not properly dressed. After four or five years with my sister and I trying to help her, we had no choice but to put her in a nursing home which was about ten minutes from my house. We visited and fed her as many times a week as we could, and finally, after being bed-ridden for three years, she passed away not knowing who or where she was. Many times, I cried at her bedside in that nursing home seeing her that old, fragile and helpless. She couldn't recognize me either during the last few years of her life.

Dad's demise

My dad never returned to the US to visit us again, after my son was about 10 years old and when he passed away, Amir was in his twenties. Dad lived with the other woman in Tehran until he passed on. He was very sick and had developed some sort of cancer. During our phone conversations he insisted that she was taking care of him. One Sunday morning, around 10 a.m. I told my husband that I had to call to talk to my father in Iran. I had never done that before as I hated calling that woman's house.

So, I called knowing that it would be around 5 p.m. in Tehran. She answered the phone and I politely asked for my father. He took a few minutes to get to the phone and was crying as we talked. He apologized for all that he had done to the family and all the pain that he had caused for all of us. I told him that no apology was needed because half a century ago someone fell in love with someone else and it didn't work between them! No matter what, he was our father and we had always loved him, and I would never forget what he had done for my children when they needed a father in their lives…

My brother received the news the next day that our father had passed away the night before, bless him.

As for me, I do wish to be able to see Iran and especially Tehran before I pass on. Apparently, Tehran has changed tremendously and if I went there I'd find it impossible to find my way around on my own. I would like very much to visit my Aunt Nour's grave, although I hear that they have been destroying most of the Baha'i cemeteries in Iran. I would love to visit my childhood town and walk through those streets one more time. I would like very much to visit my father's grave and talk to him by sitting there for a few minutes. Somewhere, I read that they called us Iranians, who had to leave everything behind and immigrate to other lands, the "Lost Generation of Iran". And I find it a very appropriate name for us.

Despite feeling a member of the Lost Generation, I have my legacy to pass on…

My Legacy

I engaged in the telling of this fragment of a life story, to share my personal legacy and connect with those who have ears to hear. My intention has been to let you know my thoughts and feelings about a tumultuous and formative period of my life. I want to honor the relationships I've formed that so greatly enriched me. I want to express my gratitude for surviving a hard yet educational life and for my growth as a person through the madness. I suppose it's possible that there could have been a version of my life where I lived without these experiences, without all of those ups and downs. Instead, my route in life enabled me to see through the surface of the world and feel through the walls that some put up to protect themselves.

I believe the adversity I endured ultimately became an opportunity for me to become my true self and find a strength I never knew existed. I learned to count on myself yet always have enough strength left to help others as well. To my mind, I learned as much as going through countless graduate programs in countless universities for the rest of my life! I became wiser and stronger when it comes to life in general. I discovered self-love and that empowered me to love my children for who they are and raise them to be independent, yet passionate people.

When I reflect upon my values and life's lessons, I realize that what I have valued most in my life is the knowledge that we as people can handle far above and beyond anything we could imagine. We are that expansive! Hard work and being one step ahead of, or flowing with, the surprises can and will do you good!

If you cannot stand behind it and say "Yes, I did it" then don't do it. Walk through life in truth, authentically showing up in complete integrity, and in the knowledge that you acted with the best of intentions for the highest good of all.

I have seen hungry cats eating frozen pumpkins on the side of the roads and hard working men who sat around one bowl of water and ate their damped dried bread as a meal. Never throw away a piece of bread; put it in a clean corner for someone or something that may need it.

My life experience has taught me that life is not like a mathematical puzzle; the outcome is not always the same. You can solve your problems by having plans and patience. The outcome may not be what you expected, but you will reach *some solution* which is better than the tangled situation from which you started! Do not try to be in complete control; that is a magic secret of life. Be organized, yes, but not to the point where you are so attached to the outcome that great disappointment can fall upon you, if the outcome was far from your expectations. Go with the flow, let go of having to be in control, and moreover, be detached from the outcome. Challenges come, but embrace them rather than resist them and the finales that arise during the steps of your evolution may well astound you. Live a life that you can look back at in wonder. Look at what you have become; or rather realize who you are. Be the co-creator of your own math!

Special memories and cherished moments

Some of my special memories are of the times that I would get up at 3 or 4 in the morning to get the babies ready to go visit their father in prison. There are sweet and sad memories held within me from those days. I was simultaneously being strong like a war machine and soft and caring as a mom during that period, which was somewhat of a dark night of the soul...

I especially cherish the moments when I was allowed to walk out of "Evin" Prison, with my two small children in my arms, after hours of interrogation. I will never forget the dense, black feeling during the moments earlier in the day as I watched the heavy metal door closing on me and the children, trapping us inside with my interrogators. The sun was shining from the left and the two little birds were pecking at the graveled road for food. Was this going to be the last time I witnessed such a beautiful sight? The angels were with me and kept me steadfast in the realm of my "enemies" in that somber place. I have since seen other sunsets and many other beautiful sights. I am confident that there are many yet to be seen.

A reflection on my spiritual beliefs

When I reflect on my spiritual beliefs, what has given me strength in difficult times is my faith in the power of goodness. So many were so good to me and my children throughout my journey during those years and I really believe it was because I have never wronged anybody in my life.

I believe in a power. I don't know whether to call it God, Nature, the energy… But I believe "God" is like a ray of sun that exists everywhere and can be reflected through all human beings. We're like mirrors for that energy/Source/goodness/power. I am spiritual, but I somehow have a bitter taste in my heart left from humanity. I used to be more positive in life and laughed more freely, loved more easily. Helping and giving to others has always been my habit, but I now keep my distance. I don't want to receive much from people because I'm not sure what they might ask in return, what their price may be if I accept anything.

Animals are far easier to get on with; with animals, you get what you see, and with people, you don't know what you're getting! There is a necessity to be careful. Half-jokingly, I used to say that I counted my fingers after shaking hands with people; I wanted to be sure that I had gotten all five fingers back! I wish I was more positive towards people, but the truth is they now scare me; they have repeatedly hurt me. I am who I am and that has never stopped me from trying to help people, but I avoid being vulnerable when I do reach out to help them.

I believe we receive or attract exactly what we spread and give away. Soften your heart and smile to others. Stay clear if you feel injustices or harm are coming your way. Remember that you don't have to like everybody and not everybody will like you in life; just don't wish harm on anybody simply because they are not your friends. Fight back like a gladiator if you have been attacked and destroy the enemy instead of just wounding them. There is nothing more dangerous than having a wounded enemy in your path. This can and will certainly involve your sub-conscious which can eat away at you, fabricating no end of paradigms that do nothing but harm or block you.

I don't know how that young girl, tottering about in high heels, turned into the woman/machine surging through, defending her children, behaving like a soldier. I have an inkling, a certain awareness of her infinite connection to consciousness. She created what she needed. She created new realities, even if she didn't like all of them at times! Now, she is more aligned to being the true her. That young girl evolved. Staying connected to the oneness that heals, she tuned into her higher self for guidance. At times she was just surviving... Gradually, she came out on the other side of the journey (which hasn't finished because it never does) onto a prettier path of joy and well-being.

An expression of regrets and forgiveness

I regret the times when I didn't spend enough time with my children, especially my little girl. I was so busy surviving that I forgot to sit with my daughter and tell her how dear she has been to me and how much I love her. I think as a successful adult she realizes that now, but I deeply regret not spending more time playing tea parties and dolls with her.

I forgive Polad, but I will never forget. He was the love of my life and he had no appreciation for me. He gambled and lost his family for what he believed was the greater cause...

I ask for forgiveness for those whom I may have hurt in my rough path to survival.

Hopes and wishes for the future:

My hopes include seeing my children finding their right life partners and having their own families. I would love to see them as parents and maybe I will get a chance in life to cradle my babies' babies in my arms a bit longer than I did for my own darlings.

I don't have any special requests to anyone for anything . . . Who would I ask? I can't ask; I never have been able to ask! Maybe that is one of my life lessons yet to be acquired...

I wish that people would see a little deeper when they look and hear more when they listen, be more aware. Do they really look and listen at all? Life can present itself as a re-run of eating, sleeping and using the bathroom over and over again, or it can be the best university that you can attend for free, by just paying attention and caring for every detail about everything and everybody, to learn and learn and learn... That is what we came here for...

Expressing my gratitude and love, I am thankful for everything that I am and I have today. There was a time in my life when I truly believed that I was the victim of injustice and there was no other person in the world as unfortunate as me. Today, when I take a hot shower I feel thankful for having hot water. When I wake up in the morning, I feel thankful for having one more day to see the world. When I see the sky I feel thankful for having my sight and when I hear music I feel thankful that I can hear. I am thankful for my children who are my resume in life by being good and hardworking people. I am thankful for being here today and feeling like a winner.

Back in 1998, when Rick and I weren't married yet. We got married in 2009 in our own backyard in the US.

Last thoughts

If I were saying "good-bye" to you today for the last time, I would want you to know that there is nothing that you cannot accomplish if you really believe that it needs to be done. May your lives be blessed with self-love and not self-pity, strength and not forcefulness and above all, with satisfaction. Always remember to expect nothing and appreciate everything, to be happy in life.

What would I like you to take away from reading this sharing? Well, that is a hard question to answer, isn't it? People take away different things from the same subject. They even see different things from the same painting. I guess it all depends on what they are looking for. I think my message to all is, quite simply, that "it could be worse"! There is always a way to make it through and doing the right thing at the same time, ALWAYS. I have no doubt about this statement and I insist on it… You don't have to become numb, as I did, to get through. Things don't happen to us; they happen through us. Be aware that all is within you, as it was in me. The numbness was an outer shell and in fact, an illusion, but the truth and strength was and is within…

End note:

As is the title of this book, so I will end this volume: Numb. In the title, as you will have realized by now, the meaning is referring to my numbness as both my sword and shield, but it has occurred to me that there is so much more to "Numb" than that. Iran is numb under the extreme Islamic regime. Ironically, that is what religion can do to a nation and its peoples, with the stories of Heaven and Hell being reflections of good and bad, as perceived by people's behavior. I say "ironically" because the meaning of the word "religion" means reuniting. We are all united by our hearts, but it seems to me that the leaders in Iran have closed their hearts and are therefore in effect Numb.

Appendix

Our House Rules while the children were growing up in the US

1) We don't lie to each other, because we know there's no punishment for you worse than hiding the truth from your loved ones.
2) We come directly back home from school.
3) We finish our homework before 6 p.m. and organize the papers in our school bag every day.
4) We put everything in the right place where it belongs. We know if it's dirty, it should go to the kitchen sink or laundry basket. If it's clean it should go in the kitchen cabinet or our closets.
5) We know that no matter how nice the weather might be, we should always ask Mom's permission before leaving the house and playing outside.
6) We consult with Mom before asking a friend to come over, or telling a friend that we'll stop over at his or her house.
7) We know that our bedtime, during the school week is 8.30 – upstairs at 8.30, lights off at 9.
8) Weekends or whenever there's no school the next day, upstairs at 10, lights off at 10.30.
9) Summer nights – upstairs 9.30, lights off at 10.
10) We don't stay outside more than maximum two hours before checking in. This means coming home and checking everything is okay. If everything is fine, ask permission for another two hours.
11) We know if we are far away from home and there's a change in our schedule, we have to call home or Mom's office to let her know.
12) We accept our punishment and try to learn something from it, not try to fight back in our own manner, when we know we did the wrong thing.
13) We're a happy, strong and complete family. We'll remain a family no matter what it takes. We're all learning a lot.
14) We also know learning is always a combination of joy and suffering. We have agreed to help each other out and stand behind each other's back, and learn how to win together. We're positive that we'll win together. Viva our family and our home.

Made in the USA
Middletown, DE
12 March 2021